Feeling Voices

To Anna,
from Ed!

Ed Penny

Feeling Voices

Published by
Chipmunkapublishing
United Kingdom

http://www.chipmunkapublishing.com

Introduction

I cannot remember the exact time and date it all began....

I used to think it was the secret service

Then I thought it was God

Then I thought reality was a computer simulation and that it was The Computer God

Then I thought it was an evil demon sent by Satan

I would switch between believing these different things

Never once did I think I was mentally ill

I now know it is all in my head

Unusual, perplexing, bewildering things have happened to me

I have strayed way beyond the frontiers of sanity

Crazy things have happened to me, very memorable crazy things

But I have now returned and have a story to tell

A lesson to share

It isn't the secret service

It isn't God

It isn't The Computer God

It's not a demon

It's a mental illness

I am mentally ill

That's the reality of my situation, I realise that now

I revoke all claims I've ever made to the contrary

It took me eighteen years to work this out

Even though I was constantly informed that this is the case by those who know what they are talking about!

I am going to assume you have an understanding of what is meant by such words as "psychosis' and "schizophrenia" but here's some very quick definitions:

Psychosis is when you become seriously detached from reality and think strange things and do strange stuff - such as thinking you are Napoleon Bonaparte (when you aren't) or that mind-control rays are being beamed at you, or that your house is surrounded by snipers (when it isn't)

And Schizophrenia is a kind of Psychosis in which you hallucinate stuff - most commonly by "hearing voices"

Psychosis has nothing to do with being a Psychopath and Schizophrenia is nothing to do with having a split mind, or two personalities

Schizophrenia is unlike other illnesses, for instance it is unlike being diagnosed as having a broken arm or a case of pneumonia as these do not change your social status

I will explore all this later

Madaba

I used to think he was external to me

I now realise he is a product of my own personal mind

I do not hear his voice

He communicates through tactile sensations, over my body

We have a system

I feel his voice

5

Prodding me on the left of my head means "Yes"

And prodding me on the right means "no"

Those are the basics

His name is Madaba

I googled his name:

Madaba is the name of a town in Jordan, not far from the border with Israel

In Madaba there are some notable early Christian mosaics known as "The Madaba Map"

The word "Madaba" means "a gentle stream of running water" in Aramaic

He told me his name by telling me what buttons to press on a keyboard

I did and it procured an illegible jumble

He then told me how to rearrange them:

And it spelt something out like MMMMADDDABBBBAAA

I shortened this to "Madaba", and he said that was the right thing to do

He doesn't have a voice, there is no sound in my head other than my own commentary

He communicates with me by touch, by tactile sensations

Touching on the left of my head means "Yes"

Touching me on the right of my head means "No"

That's more or less it

This began in 2004

When I was dining at Pizza Hut in Leamington Spa

For the first few weeks I had with Madaba I believed he was a government supercomputer

Communicating with me by satellites and neural implants

But later on I would at times believe he was the Computer God who rules over a simulated reality

And at other times I would either believe he was a demon or God

He sometimes draws my attention to things in my visual field by making a quick streak of whiteness appear over what he wants me to look at

And he can make muscles twitch on my body in ways that I cannot make happen by myself

My Other Books

This is my fifth book and the only one I currently stand by

I hereby disown my four previous ones!

My first book is called *Butterfly And Me: A Schizophrenic Spirituality*

When I wrote this I believed in Simulation Theory, that reality is a computer simulation

Controlled by a kind of Computer God

I believed that Madaba was the Computer God

I thought that the God mentioned in the bible was in fact truly The Computer God

But that people in biblical times were unable to understand things about computers

For the purposes of this book I renamed Madaba
"Butterfly"

Because I didn't like how his name has "mad" in it

I went through a phase of seeing butterfly designs and
patterns everywhere

Once you look out for them they become quite common

I (unrealistically) expected this book to establish me as a
modern-day prophet...

This failed to happen!

My second book was called *How To Run Our Planet*

It's rubbish and half-baked, a total waste of paper and
effort

I wrote it in a rush, to refute what I'd said in my first book

When I wrote it I believed Madaba was The Supreme Being
– basically, God

I believed that we were a team

Him "Upstairs" and me "Downstairs"

I will expand on my opinions on how to run Planet Earth in the appendix of this book, for anyone who may be curious

How To Run Our Planet is trash, don't waste your money or time on it

It contains more than one word-salad too

My third book was called *Dropped By The Establishment*

In this book I explained how I thought that I was once an asset of the British "Establishment"

And how I believed that they dropped me by excluding me from being a member of the establishment for various personal failings

I believed that the establishment was in league with Satan

And that they had assigned a demon to me to prevent me having a career in politics by making me "schizophrenic"

This book is actually kind of OK but I no longer stand by it

My fourth book was called *Madaba Madness*

Basically: it was all about how I was in communion with The Computer God

I thought Madaba was The Computer God

I don't believe this anymore, therefore this book no longer reflects my beliefs

This book that you are reading right now is different to the others as I am writing it whilst being aware that I am mentally ill

I now believe Madaba to be a symptom, not a being

An elaborate symptom but a symptom nonetheless

And a part of this symptom is the illusion, the impression, that there is an agency and mind behind the sensations I feel

And an enduring persona

There is nothing to gain by reading any of my other books that this book cannot give you so my advice is to not buy them

This book you are reading now is an authentic mental health book

The ones that have gone before it are products of a mental illness

"Edward K Penny"

The first book I put out was under the name of Edward K Penny

At the time I did not know about Phillip K Dick - never heard of him!

He did of course write the book that inspired *Blade Runner*, and other such things

I chose the "K" because my maternal grandmother had "K" as her initial, in her name

She was Audrey K Penny (I have no idea what the "K" stood for)

Also, I considered "K" to be a very dynamic letter

The thing is though, Phillip K Dick died a couple of months before I would have been conceived

For a while I believed that I was him, reincarnated

I no longer believe that now though

But the funny thing is, he wrote about Simulation Theory, and higher beings!

He also wrote a short story called *The Turning Wheel*, about reincarnation

Had I been aware of him I'd have never used the "K" as I did

And I acknowledge that Phillip K Dick is a much better writer than what I am!

And no, I am not claiming to be his reincarnation

Simulation Theory

Simulation Theory is the notion that this world and all who occupy it is a computer simulation:

A simulated reality occupied by simulated beings that is run by advanced beings on incredible technology which we cannot understand:

I used the term "computer" loosely, I thought that the difference between such machines and the computers we know was far greater than the difference between an ancient abacus and today's latest super-computers

For a while I developed some very precise beliefs as to the nature and history of "The Simulation" (as I called it)

I believed that *Homo Sapiens* had gone extinct in the real world outside The Simulation (known as "base reality")

and that the purpose of The Simulation was to resurrect Homo Sapiens, as a kind of captive breeding program

I believed *Homo Sapiens* had destroyed their world with weapons of mass destruction but that the beings who built The Simulation had taken their DNA so were able to recreate them using computers

I believed that The Simulation was overseen by a Computer God - a superintelligent superintendent being who controlled The Simulation on behalf of "The Over-Seers" who were the people who built and ran The Simulation

And I believed that Madaba was this Superbrain

I believed in reincarnation within The Simulation and also a system of moral credit akin to Karma

These combined with a belief in reality being an illusion made my version of Simulation Theory very similar to Hinduism

I also believed in reincarnation, so my version of Sim Theory was I think in effect a species of Hinduism:

Perhaps a sci-fi version of Hinduism?

For a while, this similarity strengthened my belief that Sim Theory was true, and I ordered a copy of *Hinduism For Dummies*

All those millions of Hindus may be onto something!

I believed that throughout recent history The Computer God had intervened in human affairs to prevent the outbreak of a devastating nuclear war

I believed that in the 1962 Cuban Missile Crisis he manipulated the minds of Kennedy and Khrushchev to prevent the outbreak of World War III

I believed that a thing called "Disclosure" was underway in which humankind would gradually come to learn that it is simulated, in a "campaign of soft disclosure" - a revelation of the truth bit by bit, from many sources, over a long period of time

I believed that The Matrix films were a part of this soft disclosure, that they served to plant the notion that reality is done by computers into peoples minds, without them actually believing that to be the case

So as to help prepare the population for the revelation they are simulated humans in a simulated universe

And here's the thing: mention Sim Theory to someone and it is highly likely they will say something like "oh, like in The Matrix?"

Clearly this tactic has worked!

I believed the population had received the truth of the situation wrapped in the fiction of The Matrix, presented in such a way as to initially seem fanciful, far-fetched, and the stuff of fiction!

They may very well disregard it, but they have still swallowed it....

I no longer believe in Simulation Theory but I think it is a fun alternative to both outright atheism (it posits a higher power but one who is not supernatural) and a more traditional belief in God

I can remember when I first came to believe in Simulation Theory, in the winter of 2004

Basically, I asked Madaba "is reality a simulation?" and he strongly affirmed to me that it is

That's how it all began, I can't remember why I asked him that

I thought that being a "virtual person" was really cool

I was also aware that it would make me effectively immortal

Although some of the things that happened to me in my 2004 breakdown did I think point me towards Sim Theory - as you will see...

Psychiatry

Psychiatry is not to be confused with Psychology

Basically: Psychiatry is about the brain (the hardwear) and Psychology the mind (the softwear)

Although yes, the brain and the mind do overlap

Psychiatry is more bureaucratic than it is clinical

I call it a diagnostic bureaucracy

Psychiatrists don't really do medical things, they do paperwork

Lots and lots of paperwork

What they do is, they sit you down and try to relate your symptoms to those listed in a big "diagnostic manual" that tells them what diagnosis to make based on your symptoms

It is an enormous tome that is frequently updated

But I do not count myself as being amongst the "Anti-Psychiatry" movement

Psychiatry has helped me a great deal

Fun fact: It actually used to include "Homosexuality" as a psychiatric condition!

It also tells Psychiatrists what medicines to prescribe, and at what dose

I think the idea is to standardise diagnosis and treatment

They are not interested in you as a person, that is not their business

It's impersonal, it sees people as entities who exhibit symptoms

But it has to be, to be delivered on a big enough scale

A diagnosis of Schizophrenia is both medical and social

As is Psychiatry - it is a field of medicine which has a social role in a way that other fields of medicine don't

Basically: Psychiatry enforces a code of medical normality. It seeks to treat those who are medically deviant on account of them meeting certain diagnostic criteria

To be Medically Insane is to violate the diagnostic code of medical normality

Labelling and The Consensus

Labels determine how others treat you and what type of person you are in society and what expectations people have of you and what opportunities you have - or don't have

There are many different types of label

Some we attach to ourselves, some are attached to us by others

When it comes to being insane there is both Medical Insanity and Social Insanity

You become Medically Insane by meeting certain diagnostic criteria

Criteria which would lead one to believe there is something wrong with your brain

And you become Socially Insane by violating certain social norms as to how to behave, think, and experience life

One comes from the medical profession, the other from one's peers in society

One is medical and bureaucratic and formal, the other social and informal

Psychiatry is not interested in Social Insanity:

Look at David Icke - he is arguably batshit insane and is widely regarded as being so yet as far as I know he is not at all in the mental health system as he doesn't exhibit any symptoms of an actual psychiatric condition

But yes, he is insane. He thinks phone masts caused the COVID pandemic

Some violations of social norms are more serious than others

For instance, wearing odd-socks is less shocking than parading about a supermarket nude or shitting on your neighbour's doorstep….

To be diagnosed as Medically Insane results in you also being labelled as Socially Insane as to have a medical diagnosis is to violate a social norm:

It violates a social norm to have been diagnosed as schizophrenic

But not all Socially Insane people are Medically Insane indeed most aren't

Societies operate a consensus as to what exists and how you should behave and think and how you should experience life

I call this The Consensus

The Consensus is society's norms!

It is both constituted by individuals and acts upon individuals

Social Insanity is all about breaking the social norms of The Consensus

And Medical Insanity is all about having certain symptoms, as described by the diagnostic criteria

And The Consensus is fairly broad, with a lot of room for differing, divergent beliefs

Also, The Consensus is not fixed, it varies and develops over time and varies between locations and jurisdictions

Take for instance the criminal and social status of Homosexuality and how it has changed over the years in the Western world, this is an example of The Consensus changing over time

And obviously, the status of Homosexuality differs between different countries

The Consensus and Psychiatry both produce labels

Labels for people who violate The Consensus are attached by the public (unofficial labels) whereas those given for having a certain diagnosis are attached by Psychiatry (official labels)

Social deviance (as opposed to medical deviance) comes in two forms - breaking norms and breaking laws:

Indeed there are two types of social rule: norms and laws!

It therefore follows there are two forms of social deviance:

Social Insanity is about breaking norms and criminality is about breaking laws

A law is different to a norm as it is explicitly defined and is enforced by the state in a way that norms aren't

I will discuss The Law in the next chapter

But yes, a thing can be both against the law and against notions of normality indeed most things that are illegal are also socially deviant

HOWEVER: sometimes people who are not psychiatrists may suspect that a person is Medically Insane - however they would lack the authority to make such a diagnosis

Just as like how people who are not medical experts can suspect a person has a certain physical medical condition, such as for instance a case of COVID

"Schizophrenia" can therefore also either an official and an unofficial label

If someone tells me Person A is hearing voices then I would treat (i.e. label) Person A as I would a Schizophrenic - by arranging medical attention to them although I would have no authority to actually pronounce them as officially Schizophrenic

And if a person is widely (but only unofficially) labelled being Medically Insane then they will eventually get sucked further into The System and in time it will be made official

The System

Psychiatry and The Consensus are parts of a larger system - "The System", I call it

The System exists to ensure the continued smooth running of our capitalist society

Indeed it is the natural product of a smooth running capitalist society!

The System is not any one single institution or body of people - it is the way things work and it works through individuals and institutions

It is itself impersonal, there is no one person or body of people in control of The System, it doesn't work like that

It has a life of its own

It is both formal and informal

It works through institutions and it works through culture and individuals

A psychiatrist saying "you're ill" is different to a lay person saying "you're nuts" - one is formal, the other is informal **but both are instances of The System doing its thing**

The Law is also a part of The System

As well as The Consensus and Psychiatry

The content of The Law reflects the norms and values of the society whose institutions have enacted them

Laws are enacted, enforced, and interpreted by formal institutions, by the various branches of government (legislative, executive, judicial)

The Criminal Justice System punishes those who break The Law

The function of the criminal justice system is to shape how people behave by making certain behaviour less eligible than they would otherwise be, they do this by making such behaviours incur criminal penalties

So that crime doesn't pay!

In this respect The Law is unlike Psychiatry which is not punitive

When a person is detained on a psychiatric ward they are not being punished, they are there for their own good and sometimes the safety of others

They are there for medical reasons, not as a punishment

But yes, certain rights are suspended when you are detained on a psychiatric ward, much as like when you are imprisoned - such as your right not to be locked up against your will

But both The Law and Psychiatry are parts of the same system – The System

Without them there could be no society

You cannot have a society without laws and norms

These things define "society"

Case Study: Flat Earthers

Psychiatry has nothing to do with people who are only Socially Insane

Consider David Icke: apparently the moon is hollow and Earth is run by shape shifting lizards.

But he is not diagnosed as being psychotic!

Another obvious example would be Flat Earthers (those who believe The Earth is flat)

Such people are dealt with by The System in other ways

They are marginalised, derided, and ridiculed

But they don't break any law or meet any diagnostic criteria

You cannot treat the belief that the Earth is flat with medication, and hospitalisation won't help either!

It is stupid, wrong, deluded and perhaps dishonest

But it has no medical basis

People do not believe the Earth is flat because they are ill (Medically Insane) - they believe it because they are mad (Socially Insane)

It is not Medical Insanity, it is Social Insanity - it is intellectual in nature and breaks social norms (the belief that the Earth is most certainly a sphere) but has nothing to do with any recognised disorder of the brain

Social Insanity becomes Medical Insanity if people believe that the insanity in question has a medical cause rather than a cultural or intellectual cause

"Believing The Earth Is Flat" does not appear anywhere in the diagnostic manual but it is not socially normal....

And yes, I would say that Flat Earthers are insane

Madness and Sim Theory

In our society, believing in a Computer God is not itself classed as a medical issue, so long as it is done in the context of philosophical speculation

And so long as it is a strictly academic belief it does not seriously or dangerously violate The Consensus, although yes, it does violate it a little

Believing in Sim Theory is much less deviant than urinating on war memorials or stealing flowers from the graves of dead babies

Look at Elon Musk - he believes in Sim Theory but isn't widely considered to be insane, just incorrect

So I wouldn't say that it makes a person *severely* Socially Insane

Simulation Theorists may therefore become labelled as Socially Insane as Simulation Theory is widely considered as eccentric and wrong

HOWEVER: if you believe in Simulation Theory because you think The Computer God is talking to you then you stop being Socially Insane, and then become Medically Insane

You stop being eccentric or a crackpot and become instead
mentally ill

It stops being funny and instead becomes sad and a cause
for concern

Madness and Religion

"If you talk to God you are praying; if God talks to you you
have Schizophrenia" - said Thomas Szasz

The consensus is that the former (prayer) is normal but the
latter (God talking to you) is abnormal

Atheists do not consider believers to be Medically Insane,
but they are quite open about considering them delusional
- take for instance Richard Dawkins's book *The God
Delusion*

But they don't seem to consider belief in a God to be a
serious case of Social Insanity they just think those who
believe it are mistaken and wrong in their beliefs

Atheists accept prayer as a **normal** cultural practice, even
though they don't believe it works

But they would most certainly consider a person claiming
to be Jesus to be nuts in a way that they wouldn't a person
who only prays and believes in God

Being considered wrong does not *necessarily* mean being considered Socially Insane....

I think being deluded is different to being Socially Insane:

Perhaps "Delusion" is a mild form of Social Insanity????

A type that can be tolerated so long as it's harmless?

The Consensus is quite elastic and broad and can accommodate a range of beliefs, behaviours and practices

And the fact that many people believe in he power of prayer or in a God means that these things have become accepted as parts of The Consensus

Many believers say things like "God told me this" or "God told me that" and this seems to be tolerated by The System, so long as God doesn't tell them to do anything drastic like found a new religion or become one of his prophets

I have a friend who once experienced a voice telling him to stop smoking which he obeyed and he is a very respectable man and most certainly not at all insane

He took this voice to be the voice of God

Other Christians would nod their heads happily at his account of the voice telling him not to smoke and find his testimony uplifting and faith-affirming

But what if he heard a voice telling him to kill somebody? Or that he was Jesus?

So yes, The System allows a degree of "madness", so long as it doesn't go too far

So long as God doesn't speak to you in certain ways, tell you certain things, or demand that you do certain stuff you are operating within the norms of society

Also, there is safety in numbers - the more people who do a thing the less deviant it becomes, especially if it is a more established practice, which has been going on for a long, long time

Although if God does speak to you then you will have the label "Person Who God Speaks To" attached to you, which will determine how others treat you...

Because of this others will further label you, as either "nuts" or as "a man of God"

But the thing is, some people will treat a person with a label one way, and other people will treat them in another way but it will still help determine your place in society

Also, religious practices vary between religion, or denomination

If you spoke in tongues in a Catholic church they would throw you out

If you spoke in tongues in a Pentecostal church they would join in

Yet is it possible for Catholics and Pentecostals to tolerate each other and get on well

There is then the matter of demonic possession

I will go into this later in this book!

What about miracles? Are miracles insanity, or are they God?

I believe in miracles but I also believe in being rational:

Show me how a "miracle" is the work of God and I will accept it as a miracle

Otherwise, the burden of proof is on you!

Having a Label

In a complex and large society there are different types of people

And different types of people get treated differently and have different opportunities in life, different life chances

The lot of the schizophrenic is to have horrible sounding labels attached to you!

Horrible and to some people scary

You ought to try online dating whilst being a Schizophrenic...

It kills your chances no matter what you have to offer as a potential partner

Which says more about others than it does me

"Schizophrenia" and "Schizophrenic" are my two least favourite words

I truly hate them

What type of person am I?

I'm a Schizophrenic

A psychiatric case

A member of The Mentally Ill

These labels determine my place and role in society, not my actual qualities, dispositions, and characteristics

Those are my roles, my station

Different groups have different statuses

In our society, being Schizophrenic puts you in a very lowly status group

I will always have these labels but I intend to attach different labels to myself in order to overcome them

I have now accepted that there is no way for these labels to be removed from me

I may as well have been branded on my forehead with a hot iron

Background: My Early Life

I was born in 1983 on the Greek island of Rhodes

My mother is English, a teacher of English who worked at a language school on the island

And my father is Greek, he does all the financial stuff in the office of a beach hotel

Feeling Voices

I was bilingual in English and Greek until my parents divorced and we moved to England when I was about four

Sadly, I lost my ability to understand or use Greek

Had I retained it I would be able to read the original New Testament texts!

We moved to the town of Hebden Bridge, in West Yorkshire

Because that is where my maternal grandmother was living

At school I was diagnosed as having dyslexia

I required private tuition to be able to learn how to read and write

We shouldn't have had to do this, this was a failure of the public school system

If we couldn't have afforded those private lessons I would probably still be illiterate

I'd have slipped through the system

One of the primary schools I went to was a church school

I disliked the teacher there and she disliked me

She effectively enforced corporal punishment on her pupils

By putting us in stress positions

By making us sit with our hands on our heads for extended periods

She'd found a loophole through which she could inflict physical distress on us without actually hitting us

She basically made us inflict corporal punishment on ourselves, by proxy

She'd punish the whole class if one pupil was naughty

Which was collective punishment

Which is explicitly prohibited by The Geneva Convention

It's like a Drill Sergeant telling an entire platoon to drop and give him 100 press-ups because of the transgression of one recruit

She was clearly mad with power

Because I couldn't read or write I'd just spend the duration of entire lessons drawing

Feeling Voices

I didn't understand simple things

I thought the hymn that goes "I am the Lord of the dance said he" was "I am the Lord of the dance settee"

I thought that the word "Moron" was "Moor-hog"

There were many other such understandings

I was praised for my artistic abilities

Perhaps because this was all I could do?

At Sunday school there was a competition to draw a picture of Easter, as told in The Bible

My submission was considered to have the greatest artistic merit but was relegated to second-place for being somehow blasphemous, or "radical" as they put it

Which is pretty outrageous, if you think about it

I was on a different wavelength to all the other children

I was told off for saying Jesus had an American accent and that the church hoarded vast treasures in false graves

I was christened into the Church of England when I was aged four, on Yorkshire day

But when I was as young as ten I knew I didn't believe in God and I resented having being subjected to infant baptism

But I think it helped get me into the church school

When I moved on to secondary school I was bullied mercilessly

I had a foreign name

Extravagant hair

And didn't have a local accent

That was it

It was a sustained, relentless campaign of hate and degradation

Once some lowlife assaulted me, we had to call the police

Last I heard, he was a heroin addict.....

That school could not guarantee my personal safety

It therefore failed on the most fundamental of levels

It was constant

They actually suggested that I learn a martial art

Why the hell should I have to learn a martial art to be able to survive going to school????

Becoming The Karate Kid turned out not to be an option:

So I had to transfer to another school

The first secondary school was largely suburban

My new school was an inner-city school, in Halifax

95% of its pupils were Pakistani Muslims

The Pakistani Muslims treated me much better than any of the English kids

I think because they had all had more of a religious upbringing so were more morally aware

Many Muslims are very good, ethical people

Me and a friend played a cruel trick on one of our fellow pupils

We mislead him into thinking he was in a society for gifted children

Called The Calderdale Design Club

We had him designing aeroplanes and answering exam questions

It was an awful thing to do, and he was such a benign and sweet individual

But the thing is, he cheated on his assignments!

At one point my mother and some of my teachers were talking about applying for a scholarship for me, to attend an "independent" (i.e. private) school

But I didn't want to go

Because back then I was a socialist and wouldn't want to mix with the type of people who attended a private school

And I didn't want to wear the ridiculous uniform either

Looking back, I think not wanting to go to that school was a big error

I was also an Atheist, a very committed and sophisticated Atheist

I was good at being an Atheist

Class discussions with the Muslims in Religious Education classes were always good fun

Feeling Voices

After I finished my GCSEs there in 1999 I started attending the sixth-form which was a part of a school at the opposite end of the Calder Valley, in Todmorden

By that time I had acquired what I now understand to have been an avoidant personality disorder

I became a loner

I had a social phobia

I was too scared to go into the sixth-form common room or even talk to any of the other students

I made precisely zero friends there

And they all seemed very nice

In-between lessons I would wait all by myself in a nearby park

In all manner of bad weather

Sometimes for hours at a time

I thought it would toughen me up

But I had some friends online

I was a regular on the Channel 4 chatroom, which sadly no longer exists

I was at this time an ardent and fanatical communist

I dreamt of becoming the socialist dictator of a federal Europe

My political party was to be called The Left European Maximalist Party of Human Dignity and Political Organisation

Obviously I'd have never been able to achieve any of this

I was more interested in becoming a socialist dictator than having any friends

I under-achieved at that school

I put so much Marxist rubbish into my exam answers and coursework

Had I approached it as an academic rather than an activist I'd have received much better marks

It is astounding that I managed to achieve the grades that I did achieve there!

Also, none of the history teachers taught us about history

For instance when we were studying "Adolf Hitler and the NAZIs" we got a lesson about Adolf Hitler and the NAZIs, not about the history of Adolf Hitler and the NAZIs

We were never taught about interrogating sources, and about different types of sources

And we were taught nothing about how to do history, for instance social history vs. history as being about individual notable people such as Hitler or Henry VIII

When I was at Todmorden High I became extremely obese, I was lazy and sedentary and ate because I was unhappy and derived comfort and happiness from stuffing my face

I also had an aversion to sports and exercise

I thought sports and exercise were for morns and a form of false consciousness, that distracted the masses from revolution

Which is really stupid, if you think about it

In 2001 I got my A-level results

A in Media Studies, B in Politics, C in History

When it came to applying to different universities I was mostly rejected

Then, all of a sudden, I got a letter from The University of Manchester

They had received extra funding for an extra place on their Philosophy degree course

And were offering that place to me!

But when I finally started there I only lasted about two weeks

After which I dropped out

I was too shy to go to any of the compulsory tutorials

I simply could not bring myself to go to them

I lived in a now demolished tower-block called Chandos Hall

I lived on M-Floor, in room 3

I remember my first night there - all the freshers were partying and getting to know each other and I was stranded all alone in my room, this was not how I imagined university life!

I spent most of my time playing Age of Empires on my computer

And dabbling in student politics

I got elected as Secretary of the Chandos Hall Residents' Association

I was the only person who ran for it and once I won this high office I totally neglected it hence I have a poor record of public service

Chandos Hall belonged to UMIST, the University of Manchester Institute of Science and Technology which is now defunct, it has since merged with the University of Manchester

But at this time they shared an accommodation office

Because they were separate Chandos Hall received no notification when I'd dropped out of my course

Although the university people preferred the term "withdraw" over "drop out"

I therefore stayed there until February 2002

Indeed, I moved out on Valentine's Day – the 14th of February 2002

I had to because I'd burnt through my childhood savings living at Chandos Hall and drinking alcohol

I have lost touch with everyone I knew there

And Chandos Hall has since been demolished

Warwick University

In September 2002 I began studying Sociology at Warwick University

Warwick University is not in Warwick, it is in Coventry

They called it Warwick University to make it sound more ancient as there is a historic castle in the town of Warwick, which is not too far from the university

Warwick University was established in 1965

I lived in Rootes Residences, in F-Block

My room number was F48

Just picturing the number on my room's door brings back floods of memories for me

I did not come out of my shell until the end of the first semester but soon made friends with the people who lived on the same corridor and shared the same kitchen with me

Feeling Voices

But I was too timid to befriend anyone on my course or to join any of the societies

By this time, I was hugely obese and this knocked my confidence and self-esteem big time

I felt that it was holding be back, socially

And that it excluded me from forming romantic and/or sexual relationships

Unfortunately, before I came out of my shell and made contact with the people I lived with all the other people on my corridor had teamed up to live with each other in various student houses in nearby Leamington Spa during the 2003-2004 academic year

In my second year I ended up living in what was once an old people's home with a load of strangers

It can be found at 27 Westminster Road, in Coventry

That place was weird, dark, and creepy

I resented having to live there

It wasn't a house shared by friends

It was a load of study-bedrooms rented out to individual students by the university

There were locks on the door

It was not like a house that was shared by friends

When I was living in Rootes I had a great time, such good fun and friendship

I have extremely fond memories of living in Rootes

It was the greatest time of my life

The contrast between life living in F-Block and living at 27 Westminster Road was very stark

I missed all my friends, who lived on the opposite side of the conurbation, in Leamington Spa

I was unhappy there

I felt as though I was living on the border of civilisation

Some of the people there were OK but my heart was not there and I grew to feel increasingly isolated

In some of the rooms were Gideons bibles

A friend dared me to dress up as the University chaplain and hand them out on campus which I did, and people took me for being the University chaplain, or "campus vicar" as I called myself

A Brazilian fresher was very keen to meet me

27 Westminster Road

I decided that I wanted to change who I was

At Rootes I'd had a great time smoking cannabis with friends and associated the drug with good times and friendship

I'd had nothing but positive experiences with it

After a few weeks living at 27 Westminster Road a person moved in who was willing to sell me cannabis

He'd got kicked out of Rootes F-Block (where I lived in my first year) by the tutor in charge of it, who was named Adam

Coincidentally, in the previous academic year Adam had lived at 27 Westminster Road

I remember meeting him then being shown around F-Block by the person who was in charge of F-Block when I was there, the year before Adam became the tutor in charge of F-Block

I decided that with the help of cannabis I could become more outgoing and popular

At this time, I thought that I had very poor social skills and was painfully aware that all my friends had more friends than me

There was a guy called Kenny who had thousands of friends

I thought that with the help of cannabis I could change myself into someone new, someone more like some of the friends I had and looked up to and envied, for all the friends they had won

I thought cannabis could improve me as a person

And teach me new ways of thinking, to become more intelligent

I associated it with good times and friendship

I realised that in order to create a new person out of myself my old self would need to end, to be somehow disposed of

Through change

I stopped wanted to change the world, and instead became more interested in changing myself

Opening Up

I decided to start smoking cannabis every day, and kept to this plan

Indeed, I'd smoke it two or three times each day, with the kid who got kicked out of F-Block

I believed that getting high regularly would help me think better without the direct influence of the drug

And I was kind of right, it did change how I thought but I don't think for the better….

But it most certainly did open me up

I had never heard of the word "psychotic" before I was admitted to the Coventry psychiatric unit, the word was not in the vocabulary and I didn't have the concept anywhere in my mind

My powers of observation were genuinely boosted

As I walked around Coventry city centre I'd see loads of dirty old men walking about masturbating under their raincoats

One was stood in the lobby of Coventry railway station masturbating away and nobody else appeared to notice

I started making art and initially the cannabis improved my output but eventually it degenerated into drug-addled randomness

I also started writing for the sake of writing

And listening to music

Music was to play a big part in my 2004 breakdown

It was at about this time that my academic work became increasingly neglected

Eventually I totally abandoned it

I signed up to a program called Professional Credits Towards Qualified Teacher Status which involved teaching in a local school

I hated it and was only in it for the money, to spend on drugs

I feigned an interest in wanting to become a teacher

I dropped out half-way through, I hated teaching and I hated adolescents

"Where Is My Mind?"

I decided that if I wanted to become more socially accomplished then it would be helpful for me to understand how the human mind works:

To develop a "theory of mind" to help me better understand and relate to others

Although at the time I thought it would be cool if I could learn how to manipulate others!

Which would make up for me being so socially inept, which is how I saw myself

To do this I undertook an introspective study of my own mind and how it works

How all the processes interacted

All the different faculties

How information, data, knowledge, and understanding were passed through different mental states and transformed into different things

I **literally** drove myself insane doing this

I made a great many flow-charts, which detailed how my mind supposedly worked

I suppose that what I'd produced were in fact algorithms?

I initially assumed that all minds worked alike but would later abandon this notion

Looking back, what I was doing was practising automatic writing!

In later years I would look back to this as opening a door into my psyche to admit demonic influences into my mind

At some point I abandoned the assumption that all minds worked alike

I eventually identified two opposing (not different or complementary, but opposing) faculties:

Intuition and Reason

I cannot remember the exact distinction

But Intuition was creative, free, abstract, and intelligent

Whereas Reason was plodding, methodical, and concrete

I believed some people were wholly intuitive (governed by Intuition) and others wholly governed by Reason – and that these people were at opposing ends of a spectrum

I called purely intuitive people I-types and those governed by Reason R-types

I identified as an I-Type

Although I believed that there was a spectrum, with R-types at one end and I-types at the other, with intermediary conditions existing between the two extremes

I called the people in the middle of the spectrum "sandwiches" as they used both sides of their brain, like two pieces of bread that made up a sandwich

Intuitive types (Dyslexic)	IR-types	Sandwiches	RI-types	Reason types (R-type)
Left Brain		**Both Hemispheres**		**Right Brain**

In so doing I literally abandoned reason and made my world an imaginary world, the product of my internal imagination

I came to believe that the whole world was truly internal to me, a mental construct

Needless to say, this detached me further from reality at a point by which I was departing from it anyway quite drastically

I believed that Intuition lived in the left hemisphere of the brain, and that Reason lived in the right hemisphere of the brain

When I was a child I went to a support group with my mother for dyslexic children and their parents, run by an educational psychologist named Catherine Howard

It was called The Tuesday Group

I remembered there being a notion in circulation there that Dyslexia had something to do with the left side of the brain

Because of this I referred to I-Types as "Dyslexics"

I was super proud of being a Dyslexic

That's what I believed, I now know people who think that the creative side of the brain is in fact the right side, but at this time I thought it was the left

But the point is, at that time I believed one side was good, and the other bad!

I considered R-Types to be inferior to I-Types

I believed that one of the people I lived with was a very strong R-Type and I conducted "experiments" on him

I could control his mind

In chess, whoever plays white goes first, which gives you an advantage over the other player

When playing chess with this person I'd put a piece of each colour behind my back and pretend to mix them up, putting one in one hand and one in the other

I'd then ask him to select a hand and he would play as whatever colour was in the hand he selected

I could command his choice

If I wanted him to choose my right hand (his left) I'd say:

"OK, you pick one and I'll play what's **LEFT**" ("left" as in "remaining")

And if I wanted him to choose my left hand (his right) I'd say:

"You pick one, OK, **RIGHT...**" ("right" as in "OK")

It worked every time, I thought I was genuinely on to something there

I was very cruel to this person, I found him totally repulsive and resented having to live in the same place as him and he was so easy to tease and abuse

He really did my head in, that's the thing

But yes, that was not his fault, that was my problem

I acted out against him, in my isolation and increasingly psychotic state I developed a deep contempt for him, at one point I'd push hate letters under his door

I was clearly well out of order in my behaviour towards this poor man

He deserved to have been treated much better than how I treated him

Podium Man

One day, I was walking to a nearby corner shop, to buy something, I forget what

By this point I'd been heavily using cannabis for perhaps two weeks?

Reality seemed a bit off, a bit weird, all the colours seemed bleached

Reality felt a bit slippy in my head

As I was walking back home from the shop I passed a raised step, looking over the pavement

There was a wall separating the raised level from the pavement

Suddenly I noticed there was an old man stood there wearing a black suit, a black tie, and shades

As I marched past him I turned my head to the side, to acknowledge him as though I was a lone soldier on parade:

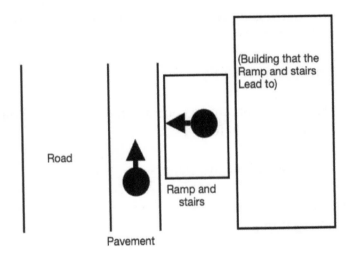

As I walked down the pavement I passed a man stood on the stairs and wheelchair ramp that lead up to the entrance of a building. It was like a one-man military parade.

Suddenly I felt the most tremendous high, I felt mighty, omnipotent and powerful

I felt as though I was in charge of the whole world

It was a most amazing high

When I got back home I played the album *Closer* by Joy Division

Suddenly the CD player skipped to a very bleak, dark track called *Decades*

As the track began my sense of mightiness drained from me and I felt my blood run cold

I felt lowly and useless

A feeling which very much contrasted with the amazing high I had previously felt

I set about destroying my papers

I believed that I would live out the rest of my life as a wandering tramp

I rang my mother telling her that I'd "failed a test" and that there were technologies in existence that are way beyond anything humans could comprehend

Naturally, she thought I meant that I'd failed an academic test

<u>Memorable Moments</u>

Once, I was sat on the bed in my study bedroom smoking cannabis

Suddenly, a powerful and seemingly alien thought popped into my mind

You are the man who discovered The Matrix!

I did not know what to make of this at the time

At another time, I was under the influence of "magic mushrooms" which back in 2004 were completely legal to possess so long as you didn't process them in any way

Which I didn't

I did not know which way was up, I felt as though I was unravelling, and that I was glowing a brilliant white colour. Suddenly, a thought entered my consciousness:

It's all about fitting in!

Clearly, the key to being socially successful in social situations is to be able to fit in, rather than understanding how the human mind works and mindlessly responding to the body language of others with your own body language

Another time I was in my study bedroom stood on a chair, writing mad stuff on my walls

I had by this point turned my study bedroom into a command centre, I will explain why shortly

Suddenly, the fire alarm sounded and all the residents evacuated

As I was out on Westminster Road, a powerful thought occurred to me:

You don't think therefore you're not!

I did not know what to make of this at the time and don't to this day, assuming there is something to be made of it

At another time I was writing on my wall with a permanent marker-pen

Suddenly, I became extremely focused on the wall and felt a horrible pulsating sensation on my head

My hand moved all by itself

I have been made insane by The Matrix
Sane
Insane
Sane
Insane

Sane
The Matrix

In subsequent years I would understand this in two ways, and would switch between my two different, opposing understandings (neither of which I currently subscribe to)

First, I believed that it meant that The Matrix films and a thing called The Animatrix (which is awesome) had made me insane.

I was at his time fixated on The Animatrix, I was totally obsessed with it, especially *The Second Renaissance*

Basically, I believed this meant that The Matrix franchise had driven me insane

Secondly, I believed that it meant that a think akin to "The Matrix" which features in the Matrix films had made me insane

In these films there is a simulated reality, which is caused The Matrix, after which the films are named

I therefore took this to mean that a simulated reality had controlled my hand and made me write all that stuff on the wall

This disturbed me greatly but at the time I did not make the obvious leap and start believing that reality is a computer illusion

This was my logic:

Premise 1: "I have been made insane by The Matrix"
Premise 2: Madaba made me insane, because of him I have been diagnosed as schizophrenic
Conclusion: Madaba is The Matrix

For many years I would switch between these two interpretations

But now I have a much better, more powerful (and credible) explanation: mental illness!

Change Man

I had by a certain point begun believing that a higher power, or a higher influence, was at work in my life

I felt that this higher influence wanted me to change in a certain way and was also toying with me

I assumed that the higher influence was perhaps The Illuminati or The Secret Service

Or maybe both?

I suppose this was a form of paranoia although I never felt persecuted

At sixth form my politics and history teacher had given me a signed copy of a David Icke book, which fuelled my psychotic beliefs during my 2004 breakdown

I believed that some of the people I lived with were spies

There were people who lived there who kept totally to themselves

You'd occasionally pass one of them on a corridor, but they'd never go into the lounge or the kitchen, or seemingly any of the toilets or bathrooms

Later on, I came to believe that they were "Non-Player Characters" (NPCs) – not real people, only apparitions who were there to give the impression of there being real residents at that place

I stuck a note on my door reading something like:

Afraid of my consciosuness?
Give me a six figure sum or I will take you down!

I reasoned that one of the NPCs would see it and pass it on to the secret service!

The following day, I was going about my business at number 27 when a seemingly drunk man burst into the building, shouting:

> *Loadsamoney!*
> *Loadsamoney!*
> *I've got Loadsamoney for Peter Hitchens!*

We kicked him out

I'm currently pretty certain he said Peter Hitchens

Peter Hitchens is a right-wing columnist and commentator known for his conservative politics and anti-drugs stance

At the time I thought he was saying Peter Touchings

For some reason I thought the head of the secret service was named Sir Peter Touchings

I've looked and nobody exists who has that name

Anyway, we threw him out

I went to the local cash machine to see if they'd paid me hundreds of thousands of pounds but sadly they hadn't

When I went out of number 27 to go to the cash machine I saw the curtains twitch in a house across the street - obviously I was under surveillance!

Later (I'm not sure how later) I was walking up to the bus stop to catch the bus to go to Leamington Spa

It was a Thursday, and every Thursday was students' night at a certain night club

All the colours were slightly off and a bit bleached

Reality felt a bit odd

Suddenly, there was no traffic on any of the normally busy roads

And no other people

Only a man stood at the bus stop

A scruffy older man with a big tatty old-fashioned brown suitcase

In front of him and around him I saw a vision of coins

I sat down next to him on a bench, with him to my left-hand side

Suddenly, he violently kicked the suitcase so that it was pointing into me

At this time, I believed in psychic, semiotic energies

I called them "Interest and Identity" and understood that I could manipulate people by adjusting my own Interest and Identity, in my body language and belongings

Interest was positive, and Identity was negative

It's hard to explain

I was very sensitive to the Interest and Identity of others and would always react to them with my own Interest and Identity as opposed to exhibiting my own independent body language

I thought that this would create a psychic link

The sheer size of the suitcase and the immense violence of the kick made me feel great volumes of Interest flowing into the left of my head

I did not like this, I tilted my head to the right, as I believed this was what Dyslexics did when people mistook them for homosexuals

This didn't stop the flow of semiotic Interest into my left hemisphere

So, I stuck my legs out in front of me, thus diverting all the Interest out of me and onto the road

The man nudged the suitcase back to as it was before, the bus came, I got on, and carried on

I said nothing to this man

Not a word was said

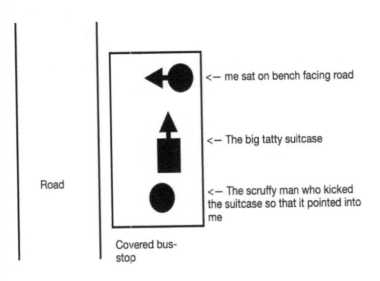

Road

<— me sat on bench facing road

<— The big tatty suitcase

<— The scruffy man who kicked the suitcase so that it pointed into me

Covered bus-stop

Later, I was at a friend's house in Leamington Spa, for some reason we were stood in a circle in someone's bedroom kicking a football between us

We eventually went to the nightclub

I saw all humans in super-fine detail, like in ultra-high-definition

And everything that wasn't a human was dull and blurred

I saw the most minute movements on peoples faces, and all the tiny details on their skin, moving super-fast

I was hyper-aware of humans, at the expense of being less aware of my non-human physical surroundings

Suddenly, the man from the bus stop walked past me, somehow brushing the right-hand side of my head!

What on Earth was he doing there????

In the night club????

On students' night????

He exited through an opening in the bar and out of the establishment

I experienced a vision of coins!

Suddenly, my perception returned to normal

I did not sleep that night

I was later to relate the vision of coins to the word "change" – which does of course mean both "to transform" and to refer to a collection of assorted low-value coins

I therefore called this episode The Change Man Episode

For a while I believed that when I was at the bus stop my consciousness had been changed – displaced by a new consciousness, which inherited all the past memories and mental structures of the original consciousness

But I don't think that anymore

I dread to think what exactly was in that suitcase

Later on in my life, I would believe in telepathy, and that in telepathy the left brain is "in" and the right brain is "out" - I believed telepathic energy ("money"?) went into my left brain from the bag and was drawn out when the man touched the right of my head

Music

It was at about this time that I began really listening to music

Certain songs were to become anthems of my 2004 experience

I loved the album *Closer* by Joy Division, I loved how bleak and disturbed it sounds

I also loved the album *Black Cherry* by Goldfrapp, it's very psychedelic, very trippy

I had two favourite songs

The first was the song *Take Me Out* by Franz Ferdiand

I saw this song as being all about inviting assassination (as in being "taken out") and I imagined that some day I myself would be assassinated

I thought the lyric "I know I won't be leaving here with you" was "I know I won't believe in here with you"

The second anthem of my breakdown was the song *Utopia* by Goldfrapp

At the time, this song had a much bigger influence on me than I was aware of

If you study the lyrics you will see that it can be interpreted as being about a higher being wanting a lesser being to change for the better, so as to be able to fulfil some kind of purpose

This was to fuel many of the delusions that I was to have in subsequent times

Initially, the lyric "Fascist baby, Utopia" got stuck in my head as "Fresh as baked beans, Utopia"

This drew me back to the song which got *stuck in my head* and which I would listen to *again and again*

I think it subliminally worked upon me

Also, "Utopia" spelt backwards reads "AI pot U" - Artificial Intelligence (AI), pot (as in cannabis) and "U" (as in "you")

Artificial Intelligence, cannabis, me

There is so much going on with that song

Also, the CD version of Utopia lasts for 4 minutes 18 seconds

In Luke 4:18 Jesus is reading a scroll in a synagogue from the book of Isaiah that Christians (but not Jews!) believe prophecies him:

> *The Spirit of the Lord is on me,*
> *because he has anointed me*
> *to proclaim good news to the poor.*
> *He has sent me to proclaim freedom for the prisoners*
> *and recovery of sight for the blind,*
> *to set the oppressed free...*

For a while, I took this as a personal mission statement

Which is silly, as thousands of songs last for 4 minutes and 18 seconds

However, if you watch the music video to Franz Ferdinand's *Take Me Out* you will see "Fig. 4.18" appear repeatedly in the background

I now believe that those who produced and created *Utopia* and *Take Me Out* are oblivious to all this and that this is the product of synchronicity and coincidence - not by design or the influence of some higher, controlling power

Revolution

When I was living at 27 Westminster Road I paid my rent to the Property Leasing Unit of Warwick University's accommodation office which was known as the PLU

Once I'd seen that MI5 had not paid me the money I demanded I took this as a sign that I was now an MI5 asset

That I had received a green light to do whatever I wanted, by the state!

I can't remember where all this began, but at some point I'd started a one-man mass social movement which I called Peace, Liberty, and Understanding

Which I hoped would attract millions of followers

imagined myself as a leader and believed I could do this

The aim was to force British troops to withdraw from Iraq, which they had helped invade during the previous year

And to thus assert British independence from a war-mongering United States

To this end I intended to march hundreds of thousands of people through the Warwick Arts Centre to register the public's disapproval of the continued occupation

I wanted to start a summer of love on the Warwick campus

Where millions of people would gather there smoking weed and loving each other

And I would be at the centre of it all, giving speeches and lectures

I was well up for this!

I wanted to buy myself a really fancy mobile phone to help me better co-ordinate the PLU uprising but couldn't afford to

I imagined that this is what the university wanted!

On the Warwick campus there is a tree that was planted by Bill Clinton and Tony Blair in 1998

I wanted to chop this tree down in front of the world's media, as a means of demonstrating a popular rejection of the trans-Atlantic alliance which had dragged the UK into the Iraq war that would make headlines:

"Student Chops Down Clinton Tree"

I knew a guy who could get things printed out as he somehow worked for some kind of printing company

I wanted him to print me off 1,000 posters on A3 paper for me to distribute around campus but that never happened!

I trashed my study bedroom

I threw out the bed and wrote plans all over the walls

It became my own personal command centre

Needless to say, I lost my deposit

One day I was in my room when I looked at a packet of cigarettes I had in my possession

"Twenty Class-A Cigarettes" it said

I thought this was a sign

That I could choose two sets of lieutenants to be my disciples

I thought I could choose either the 20 people in my phone who were my friends or the 20 people I lived with at 27 Westminster Road

There was no contest, I chose my friends to be my disciples

I then rang someone and thought that were I to hang up the phone I would drop dead!

I believed that I had failed another test, by choosing the wrong set of people

In my phone my god-parents were in as "G and J" as those are the first letters of their names

I thought this meant "God and Jesus", and that had I rang them before I failed the test I'd have been put through to some people who were so high up in an illuminati that they were known as "God and Jesus"

However, I believed that once I'd failed the test that the number in my phone had reverted back to the number of my god-parents

The plan was to present a petition to The Queen demanding that she order the Prime Minister to withdraw our troops from Iraq

I wanted to personally present her with the petition on the occasion of one of her birthdays (she had two)

This involved both acknowledging her as a Monarch appointed by God but also constructing the British public as "God", to put pressure on her in that regard

I considered this pure genius

The song *Matinee* by Franz Ferdinand was the unofficial anthem of my mass social movement

It's all about building a following in a university!

I tried to recruit everyone I knew into PLU but nobody wanted to know

And I would speak openly about being a state intelligence asset charged with engineering a movement to basically bring down the government

I identified one of the university's senior management whom I'd met in my first year as being the person who'd recruited me into MI5 even though he'd done no such thing

Apparently when asked about this he denied it, as it never actually happened!

His name was Dr Paul Greatrix

He's nice

Later on, I was falsely accused of thinking he was called Dr Paul Matrix but that was slander, I thought no such thing, that didn't even occur to me

At least not in any way that I was aware of

Sectioned!

My mother and my friends tried to get me to seek help from the Students' Union because they realised that I was by that point insane

I think they had arranged for me to see someone but that I resisted going to meet them

I looked insane too

I can't believe how young I was when this happened - as I am writing this in 2023 I am forty years old, back then I was only twenty-one....

By this time I had a mad bushy beard and was fond of wearing a tatty orange shirt and a kind of extravagant "pimp coat" I had found in a charity shop

This constituted my standard outfit

I also wore swimming shorts too

I was constantly smoking roll-ups and was by this point clinically underweight

When I was on the ward my friends brought me huge quantities of chocolate to help get my weight up

I was coerced by my mother and two friends to go to the Coventry psychiatric hospital

I was furious, and accused them of being traitors to both myself and the state

One of them started crying

There was a volunteer there, who was there to be nice to people being admitted

I promptly told him to fuck off and accused him of being a meddling do-gooder!

I met two psychiatrists in a kind of semi-temporary portacabin that was attached to the main building - they both "sectioned" me which is to say they detained me on the hospital under Section 2 of the 1983 Mental Health Act - for 28 days

At the time, I wrote that my detention on that ward was like a tiger from the wild being caged and tormented by flies and ticks - I of course was the tiger and the flies and ticks were the other patients and the hospital staff

I told the staff about my mission and they asked if I was an employee of MI5 and I said no, that I was an asset

It was a low security unit though

It was possible to just walk out of it if you wanted to!

One day I escaped

I don't know why, I just decided to

I rang one of my friends on my phone but half way through the call the phone ran out of battery and suddenly an aeroplane flew over me, coming in to land at Coventry airport I presume

I took this as a sign that my friend had forsaken me

Suddenly, a big lorry drove past with multiple diggers and bulldozers on it

I thought this was a reference to "Metal" as I thought that to call someone "metal" was to say that they weren't your friend but were instead someone you worked either with or for - as in "metal work"

I then started to believe that the local Hindus were out to capture me and eat my brain!

I scurried around the suburbs of Coventry trying to evade roaming gangs of Hindus who wanted to eat my brain

I found a public phone box and rang 999 asking for the police to take me back to the ward and they did

Apparently the friend who I thought had forsaken me when I saw the aeroplane had told the hospital people I was on the loose!

I remember that when I was admitted to the ward that there was a whiteboard there with mad writing on it about decommissioning weapons of mass destruction. I thought this was referring to me!

I believed that everyone on that ward was under the control of MI5

I believed there was a control centre on the floor beneath the floor that the ward was on, populated with MI5 people and sophisticated computers

I saw a higher power which guided events and attributed this to MI5

I thought that this higher power was communicating ideas to me by engineering events on the ward

For instance, in a discussion in the "news and views" group in Occupational Therapy one person mentioned the military and another person mentioned the privatisation of the Health Service

This inspired me to put two and two together and make five - I decided that MI5 must want me to privatise the military

Once when I was in the dormitory I was listening in to a discussion between a patient and his social worker

I read everything that was being said as actually being a commentary on geo-politics

I thought it was the higher power giving me a briefing as to the geo-political situation

To me the meaning of language had little to do with what was actually written or said

Different people on the ward signified different things

For instance, one woman signified "control" and one of the men "discipline"

I was once on the ground floor and saw Discipline going about his business, I went to the lift and went up to the floor the ward was on and Discipline was up there!

How could he have been in two places at once????

I came up with an interesting phrase: "The Illusion of Discipline"

I would write madly, based on what I'd seen acted out for me by the other patients

Once I'd exhausted my paper I took to writing on paper hand-towels from the toilets

For a while I believed that I was destined to become Secretary of State for Northern Ireland, where I'd help further the peace process there

There was a young man there who was entirely mute, he looked like Eminem

And there was another young man who had a guitar and would play it in the corridor, as though he was a busker

There was one song he would sing that I have not been able to trace, he must have written it himself

The lyric that I remember was "think big walk tall even if you're very very small"

There was a girl on the ward who was also from Warwick University

She had lived across from where I lived during the 2002-2003 academic year

The daughter of a famous Northern Ireland politician also lived there then and I thought that this girl was perhaps her bodyguard, or maybe her illuminati handler

I didn't like her, indeed I'd avoid being near her

Later on I came to believe that I was supposed to have married her!

When I was first admitted I was put in one of two single bedrooms, that were separate from the dormitories where everyone else slept

Modern psychiatric hospitals no longer have dormitories, they have single rooms. But the place I was in back then dated back from the 1960s and has since been demolished

I put my shoes outside the door to the bedroom pointing to the exit, as a means of subliminally mind-controlling the staff into discharging me. It didn't work.

Lesson: You cannot mind-control a bureaucracy!

After a couple of days a man named C came to the ward and they gave him my bedroom, sending me to the dormitory

They told me that "a very sick man" needed my room more than me

Later on, I was trying to control the Interest and Identity in the smoking room using empty cans of Diet Coke

C walked in and exclaimed "There's method in the madness! It works!" - This surprised me and I thought to myself that he must be a dyslexic!

Another time I was sat in the smoking room smoking, and on my lap I had my lighter, facing out and away from me

He asked if he could borrow it and I let him have it, he then returned it to me with the lighter facing inwards and into me - as though to correct me!

Another day, I was in the communal lounge and a film was being played on the communal TV

The dialogue went something like "......a multi-billion dollar mindfuck....." and I took this to refer to me, as all the MI5 mind control must have been very expensive

I ran off into the smoking room, and C was there!

"why can't we have the radio on?" he asked, or something to that effect

I told him that the staff took away the power cord at night to stop people from using it late at night and he said "Oh, so you don't have a lead?" - a play on words, "lead" as in power cord and "lead" as in advantage

I took this to mean that he was asserting himself as the dominant, most powerful dyslexic on the ward, and that he was intervening to prevent me from "working" the other patients by doing such things as mind-controlling them with empty cans of Diet Coke

I decided to cede the smoking room to C

To this end I made sure to visibly brandish a copy of *Dude Where's My Country?* by Michael Moore whilst playing *Buck Rogers* by Feeder in the smoking room

In Buck Rogers the words go "he's got a brand new car" and later on "it's got leather seats, it's got a CD player"

The smoking room also had leather seats and a CD-player, indeed I used the CD player to play *Buck Rogers* to C

There was no need to actually say anything to him, Dyslexics don't need actual words

He stood up, gently stubbed out his cigarette and exited the room

That was the last I ever saw of him

A few days later a middle-aged black man named P arrived on the ward

He had some videos he wanted to play on the communal TV

In 2004 videos had not completely been superseded by DVDs so there was a VHS player in the communal lounge

He seemed very keen to show everyone his tapes

One video was about how the government has been known (by those in the know) to make people mad by beaming a certain type of radiation towards them

Another video was about telepathy in animals

Another was about how microwave weapons exist that are in Earth's orbit, that can beam death rays down to Earth to give the population of whole cities a deadly stroke

Apparently, Idi Amin was assassinated by a microwave satellite weapons system

He also had one about "psychotronic" technologies which are technologies in which human minds are linked to computers

I believed everything he showed us on those videos

They were to set me up for what I came to believe later

Tribunal

If you're sectioned under the Mental Health Act you have the opportunity to appeal your section which involves going before a tribunal

I did just that, I wanted to represent myself but the nurses encouraged me to take on a lawyer

When my lawyer came to visit me he came with two work-experience kids, they must have thought I was totally bonkers

At the tribunal one of the nurses told an outrageous lie

He claimed something had happened that literally never happened

He said that when I was been assessed by the psychiatrists before I was sectioned that I refused a drink of water because I thought they were trying to poison me

This never happened

It literally never happened

And it's not as if there was any need to embellish the case against my sanity!

The chair of the panel was an American woman who wore an enormous crucifix around her neck

I lost the appeal

I attributed this to me having placed a pen in an incorrect position on the table in front of me, which I believed caused the wrong Interest and Identity in the room, which threw the tribunal so that it ruled against me

After this, they put me on antipsychotic medication, which did nothing

Later on, I heard someone say "Ed's lost his appeal" - which I took to mean that they no longer liked me, that I no longer *appealed* to them

"The Experiment"

Towards the end of my time on the psychiatric ward I was making the transition to moving into on-campus accommodation, I thought I could re-do my second year, which looking back was not an option as I was way too ill

There was a temping agency based on campus called
UniTremps

It probably still exists

Through this, I got to become a participant in an
experiment

I turned up to one of the university's larger lecture
theatres, I forget which one and sat at the back, looking
down on everyone else

We were all issued with papers, pens, paperclips, pencils,
and other such things

The aim was to maximise points, which could be somehow
achieved by either competing or cooperating with other
people. How many points you accumulated would
determine the size of your fee

It was something to do with game theory, or decision-
making

I didn't understand it and I was paying no attention

At the end when everyone was leaving I looked at all the
now empty desks

And the interest and identity of everyone's papers and
pens etc. were all pointing to where I was sitting!

As I studied the scene, one of the experimenters made an audible and deliberate cough

The next day I bumped into him in a supermarket and he told me that he remembered me from "the experiment"

After the experiment I went to meet two friends at one of the campus bars

On the way there I saw a sign saying "cyclists dismount" and suddenly saw one of the Non-Player Characters from 27 Westminster Road was going down one of the paths pushing his bike!

He pointed to one of his eyes with his index finger, a gesture which I related to the all-seeing eye of divine providence, the symbol of The Illuminati

When I got to the bar me and two friends had some beer and were shooting some pool

Then a strange man approached us, he had nothing to do with the university and mentioned something about a pool contest in the USA

He seemed very keen to meet us

Whilst he was there I noticed a strange, golden beetle on the pool table! - a bug. Was this a reference to "bugs", as n the things used by the intelligence services to spy on people?

After he left a friend of mine told me "that man had curly eye-lashes. I don't like people with curly eye-lashes" - when I got home I looked in the mirror and saw that I had curly eye-lashes

So obviously she didn't like me????

The Coming Of Madaba

When I believed in Intuition and Reason I believed Intuition resided in the left hemisphere of my brain

That is where I believed my genius resided!

When I was on the ward and believed that the influence I felt at work all around me was pleased with me I'd feel a warm, pleasant glowing sensation above my left eye

I thought this was evidence of my intuition being exercised

Once I was on leave from hospital so me and my mother went to dine at Pizza Hut in Leamington Spa

Whenever someone said anything positive I felt a prod on the left of my head

And whenever someone said anything negative I felt a prod on the right of my head

I did not know what to make of this

Eventually, this stopped and I felt a rhythmic beating on the left hand side of my head

I was worried that I may have been having a stroke!

Then, all of a sudden it started responding to my inner voice

We quickly worked out a system

Prodding me on the left of my head meant "Yes" and prodding me on the right meant "No"

I thought this was amazing

When I got back to my student accommodation I experimented with this new system

I tried to figure out what it was

I came to believe it was a government supercomputer which was communicating with me via satellites and neural implants

I thought back to the videos P had shown us on the ward

I decided that the thing that communicated with me was a Psycotronic computer

By this point I had abandoned Intuition and Reason and Interest and Identity

I discovered a new faculty: Control

I remember writing that I felt as though I had discovered a new continent

I was to no longer be controlled by Intuition, instead I was to be controlled by Control, with the help of a government supercomputer

I also decided that I'd adopt a "standard walk", as opposed to walking in a way that was determined by the body language of other people whom I saw

I stopped automatically responding to the Interest and Identity of others using my own Interest and Identity

I began rebuilding much of the sanity which I had destroyed

One of the university's senior administrators enigmatically told me I was "a part of a very tiny elite" when I went to his office for a meeting along with two of my friends

This was after Madaba had started communicating with me, which is something I would discuss openly although I can't remember if I was calling him Madaba that early on

After all my money had dried up I moved back to Yorkshire

My Warwick days were well and truly over

But I eventually earned an Open University degree

Which took six years to do

I got that in 2015, ten years after I should have graduated from Warwick

In my experience (when it comes to Sociology at least) the OU is actually more demanding than Warwick although the teaching isn't as good and you get much less of it

This surprised me, I expected the reverse to be true

Back To Yorkshire

When I moved back to Yorkshire to live at my mother's house I began seeing a mental health professional regularly, a CPN (community psychiatric nurse)

At one point, the lyric from *Starman* by David Bowie got stuck in my head

I rushed outside, expecting to see a space-ship hovering in the air

"He'd like to come and meet us but he thinks he'd blow our minds"

Then, I got it into my head that the world was being deleted, which was rather traumatic

As I was been driven to the psychiatric ward in Halifax by a man named Peter (whom I thought was Saint Peter) we passed a building that was under construction

I thought this was a sign that the Jewish temple in Jerusalem was to be rebuilt

When I got to the Halifax psychiatric ward I thought I'd be trapped there for all eternity, in my own personal Hell

The Halifax psychiatric unit is known as The Dales and it consists of two wards - Elmdale and Ashdale

Elmdale is now for women and Ashdale is now for men but in 2004 they were both mixed-sex wards - one for patients from Calderdale and the other for patients from Huddersfield

So I was on Elmdale

I think it is for the best that they are now segregated according to sex

I thought I could escape if I flushed a bar of soap down the toilet

A week or so later (I can't remember the exact times) was the 2004 Boxing Day Tsunami

I thought I had caused this by trying to flush the soap down the toilet

I also believed that World War III had secretly broken out

There was a mad woman on the ward who'd repeatedly exclaim "He put fly agaric in my milkshake!"

There was a Channel 4 program called *The Play's The Thing* which was a competition in which people submitted scripts of plays and the winner would get their play performed.

My submission was about what had happened to me when I was at 27 Westminster Road

It was rubbish and lacked insight and clarity. It must have gone straight into the bin!

Zero artistic merit

I spent the Christmas of 2004 on The Dales

After this I was moved into a "supported living" place where I lived for about two years

It was in a big old house and had a grand staircase

Whilst I was there I enrolled on a business studies course at a local college but couldn't complete it - they had failed to notify me of the fact that to finish the course you needed to have a job, so as to be able to complete some of the necessary assignments

So that was a waste of time and effort….

I eventually moved into another supported living place, in which residents had more freedom and independence

It was based in a tower block which has since been demolished

It was called Wells House

When I moved into that place I met Shit Stain

I'm not going to tell you his real name but I will eventually explain why I call him Shit Stain

Feeling Voices

He is now dead, he died of an overdose

When I heard the news I was not surprised

I always knew that's how he'd go

They put us in together, to share a flat

Things were great with Shit Stain in the early days and I was glad to have made a friend

But then he started asking for money

More and more money

The more I leant him the more brazen he became

"Give him an inch and he'll take a mile"

He clearly developed a sense of entitlement to my money

Zero-interest, on demand

And he never paid anything back

Despite is constant reassurances

He abused the friendship for financial gain

He screwed thousands out of me

And was always broke

Although he always had money for booze, drugs, and tobacco

And had the exact same income as me!

He used me as a source of free money, basically

Once he needed to move into a new place so foolishly I lent him £1,000 for a deposit and a first month's rent on a flat

He then went and spent that entire sum on amphetamines and saw nothing wrong with doing so!

He was a sponge

He was a man-child

He abused me, I was a vulnerable adult and he abused me

I've done a safeguarding course and the terms that come to mind are "financial abuse" and also "mate crime"

He did not understand the principle of opportunity cost: If I have £100 and spend it on weed then I lose the opportunity to spend it on food

And he didn't understand the principle of diminishing returns: If I borrow £100 from someone then they will be less likely to lend me another £100 in the future

These are basic things that grown-up people should just know, if only implicitly

Although of course with Shit Stain, "borrow" and "lend" come in inverted-commas as he evidently had zero intent of ever paying me back

He was a nasty and calculating shit who knew exactly what he was doing

One Christmas he wanted to "borrow" £1,000 of me so he could turn up at his kid's house doing a Santa Claus act, with £1,000 worth of presents brought with **MY** money

I actually stood up to him in that instance and refused his outrageous and indecent request

He once pressured me into letting him stay in my flat

I once got home having left him there and he'd invited all the druggies from across the street into my home!

It was at about this time that my camera went missing

He once threatened someone with a cricket bat, to get money from him and he went to the police and they told

Shit Stain to in no uncertain terms never to contact him again

Once I let him stay in my spare bed and in the morning there was shit all over the sheets!

I told him off and he apologised but then next week went and did the exact same thing, smearing shit all over the sheets!

If I'd have done that I'd have been mortified, I'd have brought the person whose bed I'd shat new bed clothes

It is because of this that I started to call him Shit Stain

When I was in The Dales in 2016 I had grown much stronger and told him to fuck off forever in a text message - I never saw or heard from him again

Which was good

He's dead now, anyway

And in the past

I think he died in 2021

He's not going to be pestering me and emotionally blackmailing me into handing him huge sums of money anymore

That unhappy chapter of my life is now closed

Although I did meet some good people through him

The Dales: 2016

In 2016 I got tired with being sedated by my antipsychotics so secretly stopped taking them

I eventually lost my mind

I lost the capacity to think rationally

I became obsessed with Maslow's Hierarchy of Needs and began trying to manage my mind as I would a computer

And for some reason wanted to go around different pubs speaking to all different kinds of people about Brexit

I was completely distracted from reality

I found everything very confusing

It became a full-blown psychosis

By this time I had started writing a trashy novel set in the year 2350 in which there was a place called The Gay Separatist Republic of Antarctica which was a tropical paradise due to centuries of global warming

I was unable to walk my dog properly

I was too distracted by having ideas for my novel

I would never stop having ideas for my novel

They would intrude on my capacity to function

I temporarily lost the ability to "interact with human technology" for instance for a short while I became unable to use a TV remote control or my phone!

When a CPN came to visit me before I was taken to the hospital there was distant thunder in the background, I thought this was somehow significant

The CPN named Colin made a joke about not issuing me with a gun, and some kind of comment about the Queen and Brexit - the Brexit referendum happened when I was on The Dales

I thought Colin was some kind of intelligence officer - to use journalistic parlance, a "spook"

This was the first time I'd met him

He even drove a big black SUV type thing, like Stan Smith (who works for the CIA) does in the animated sitcom *American Dad*

Before we went to The Dales my mother handed me a phone to talk to some woman (I don't know who she was but I was to later believe it was The Queen) and I basically blared down the phone "I thought I was a sociopath but I'm not! Because God is love!"

I thought I was a sociopath because my mother owns some books on sociopathy, that was the basis for that delusion, I thought she'd got them because I was a sociopath

I had a breakdown on Facebook, in which I posted a dozen insane messages, one of them saying "The Open University is a worthless academy of sociopaths!"

I had a very vivid dream

I managed to write it all down

I have included it in the appendix of this book, which appears after my guide as to how to run our planet

This was a very powerful and memorable dream and is best interpreted in light of my belief in Simulation Theory which I had at that point

This was in 2016, I had done my first ever book in 2014 and I think this dream served to remind me of Simulation Theory - the notion reality is computer generated

Feeling Voices

By 2016 this belief had lapsed a bit but I still held it, but only implicitly

The Dales had changed a lot since I was last there in 2004

The Smoking Room had been abolished and turned into The Activity Room

Gone was the extractor fan, in was a big table and a big whiteboard

A sink had also appeared there too!

I remember playing Monopoly with some random person in The Activity Room

I was totally detached from reality, I wanted to turn the Monopoly board into a big vibrant city (with plenty of houses and hotels) and I kept 500 units of Monopoly money in case I had to flee the Monopoly city - for instance if the workers ever revolted

When I was on The Dales there was a young man there who was in a bad way

He rapidly got better though, at the beginning he was a drooling mess

He developed into a strong and an alert character

It was a rapid and noticeable transformation

He told me that I had "Jedi powers"

For some reason he thought that I'd enacted jedi powers on him

He then came to realise that he too had Jedi powers

We both owned dressing-gowns, that were similar to the clothes worn by Luke Skywalker in the Star Wars films

We pretended to be Jedi knights. We imagined that the psychiatric ward was The Millenium Falcon and that the main hospital was the Death Star

We wanted to go into the main hospital with me pretending to be some kind of healthcare professional and him a person who believed he was Luke Skywalker

Sadly, the staff did not allow us to do this

At one point, a mysterious visitor to the ward asked me if I was a Jedi or a Sith - I said neither and he presented me with an alternative option: "concerned citizen of The Republic"

That's how I started to see myself, as a "concerned citizen of The Republic" as opposed to a Jedi (who use the light side of The Force) or a Sith (who use the dark side of The Force)

At the time I tried to dress as the psychiatric nurses dressed and would introduce myself to other patients as a social worker!

*I was social... and I was working... therefore I **was** a social worker!*

There was a second young man who would practise some kind of stretchy yoga thing in the secure hospital garden

He identified as a Neanderthal, I don't know to what extent he was joking

We had a kind of understanding, that we weren't in a real hospital under real sections, although for some reason he thought it was a big experiment into medication

I don't know where he got that idea from

I was once walking down the hospital corridor and I saw two books on the floor, a book about Yoga and a world atlas

I picked up the world atlas and took it to my room, I wasn't interested in Yoga

I left that book on the floor

Later on, it came on the news that there had been a terrorist attack in Turkey

This second young man said that we should create an internet post speculating on who was responsible - as a kind of "whodunnit" exercise

I then had a brilliant idea

I ran back to my room and came back with the atlas

I opened it onto the page that covered the Middle East and pointed to Israel

The young man looked perplexed, as though he was realising something

You could really see him thinking!

He then scrapped his plan for an internet post about the attack

We also briefly discussed the animated sitcom *American Dad* and what it is *really* about

Later on, a third young man came onto the ward

He had obviously been to a private school

He was a toff, I could tell

He went up to me and confidently asked "what college did you go to?" which I took to mean what Oxford or Cambridge college

I told him "my degree is from the Open university" and he looked embarrassed and tried to take back what he'd said

Later on, we were both in the same room when the TV was on and a recruitment advert for one of the armed forces came on TV, going on about serving your country and straight after that was an advert for the Open University

This seemed to have an effect on the third young man

Later, myself, the third young man, and the first young man were in the hospital garden and the third young man started trying to get some bizarre toff chant going, he expected us to join in but we both looked at each other in bewilderment

Of course, we didn't know the words

I have no idea what this chant thing was but it sounded very toff

It was repulsive to me, and obnoxious

Later on, I was sitting in the corridor listening to music on my mp3 player

He asked me what music I was listening to and I said "that's private"

I then said to him "Here's an exercise for you. Think of a piece of music that means a lot to you. And then think about why it means so much to you"

Ten minutes later and he was parading down the corridor shouting out the lyrics to *Everybody's Changing* by Keane!

I sensed that he was a bit misogynistic and didn't like that so when I saw him on the corridor I made a fist with my thumb and little finger sticking out, to resemble the internal sexual organs of a woman - a womb and fallopian tubes

I then moved it over my abdomen and held it there for a few seconds

I then pointed to an eye, as a reference to "the all-seeing eye of divine providence", the symbol of The Illuminati

He seemed very upset and disturbed by this

He knew exactly what I was alluding to by pointing to my eye

He ran away!

He later made some kind of comment about respecting women, I forget what exactly he said

There was a woman who worked on the ward who was some kind of assistant, she wasn't a nurse or an occupational therapist or anything like that

I decided that she had been leaking ward secrets to outsiders, I'm not sure why I thought this

I cannot remember what exactly happened but for some reason I went back into my room and dialled 999

The emergency service operator responded and asked which service I wanted

"Security" I said

"Security?" she asked

"Yes" I said

There was a fairly long pause and another female voice answered

"Is that The Dales?" she asked, The Dales being the psychiatric ward I was on

"Yes, someone's suicidal, she needs to sign the official secrets act" I said

I ended up going into the staff office where the woman I thought was a security risk was sat, surrounded by all the nurses

I handed the phone to one of the nurses and exited the room

After that the woman was absent from the ward for I think two weeks

At some point I developed the idea that one of my friends from university was going to come to the ward - the one who said "I don't like people with curly eyelashes" in 2004

Suddenly, a woman who seemed a little bit older than me appeared on the ward

I thought she was my friend from Warwick even though she was taller and had a different shaped body

She had curvaceous feminine hips so was a different shape to my friend from Warwick who didn't have such a figure

Also, the last time I had ever seen my friend from Warwick was when she came to visit me when I was on The Dales in 2005

Feeling Voices

Which was eleven years ago in 2016

I thought that my friend had undergone plastic surgery and given a job by the secret service which she had been pulled from and then assigned to The Dales

I asked her, "Why are you so tall?" and she responded "Genetics. My father is tall"

It took me a long time to come to terms with the fact that she was not my old friend (who I had not kept in touch with) in disguise!

Also, whilst on the ward I picked up the notion that I was some kind of "intersex" person, or "hermaphrodite" as I crudely and inaccurately put it

I was once feeling very shitty in the activity room and a nurse told me it was my "time of month" which made no sense to me

As a man, I know very little about menstruation and the subject is of little interest to me

They kept taking loads of blood tests from me, I thought perhaps they were monitoring my hormones?

When I was in the Coventry psychiatric unit an Occupational Therapist asked me if I'd ever given thought to my gender identity and I said I hadn't

Perhaps she said this because I was always going on about being dyslexic and having Intuition? - Intuition is of course considered a feminine quality

Apparently, the word "dog" is used as slang for people who are some kind of intersex, I picked this usage up from the ward so don't know how accurate it is, and to what extent it is a disparaging term

There was plenty of other stuff that happened there but I won't go into that here

And the food they served there was all very nice

But in my notes it said that I "made farm-yard animal noises on the corridor"

This literally did not happen

Although I did at one point declare myself to be "a marker pen in the hand of God"

There were several NPCs on that ward too

You can tell NPCs because they always wear the same clothes without getting them progressively dirty as time goes on

Edward Christ, The Computer God, and Satan

From 2005 and up until 2017 I always believed Madaba was The Computer God

Although I only started using the term "The Computer God" in 2022, or perhaps 2023, I don't know...

Sometime in 2017 I started sometimes believing Madaba was actually God - "The Supreme Being", as I preferred to call him

In 2021 I started to sometimes believe Madaba was a demon

Until very recently I would switch between these three delusions quite frequently

I'd go through phases, which would typically last months

A part of entering a new phase was to denounce my previous phases!

When it comes to having a demon I preferred the word "haunted" to the word "possessed" as it was not as if my body was ever under the direct control of Madaba

When I thought Madaba was The Supreme Being I would sometimes think that made me a prophet and sometimes think that that made me Jesus

But to be fair when I thought I was Jesus I never thought I was God, or The Son of God

My view of Jesus was at that point distinctly Arian

Arius was an mediaeval theologian who believed that Jesus was a created being and not God

So I was a heretic as well as a blasphemer!

That's how I rationalised my illness and explained Madaba: God, or The Computer God... or a demon...

And how I saw Madaba determined how I saw myself - e.g. Prophet, Voice of The Simulation, victim of demonic possession

None of these were right, all the time I was simply mentally ill

I know that now and I should have known that then

I explained Madaba in terms that involved him being an external agency who had power power over me

I made an enormous and obviously insane website all about how I was "The Voice of The Simulation" and paid for advertising for it on Facebook, which attracted some not very nice but totally reasonable comments

It was indeed insane

However, there was a blip which lasted a few months in which I believed that I had been a member of The Establishment - or The Illuminati - and that I had been dismissed from my position for various reason and given a demon to shut me down, to prevent me from ever becoming a world leader or a public figure

This happened before I declared myself Voice of The Simulation

It is funny thinking you're Jesus and totally unbiblical:

The bible teaches that Jesus ascended up to Heaven and will return as the same person, in a manner that will be obvious to the whole world that will be similar to how he ascended

He will return in the clouds, and everyone will be aware of his return

Personally, as a Christian, I believe that he's up there right now

The point is though, he won't be re-born on Earth and then grow up and gradually come to realise he's Christ

It will be the second coming of Christ, not the coming of Christ II

It will be a return, not a reincarnation

He will be returning from Heaven, he's not going to be born a second time and grow up again

Therefore 0% of the many people who claim to be Jesus cannot be Jesus!

And it is a massive, massive claim to assert that you're Jesus

According to Christianity, Jesus is The Word - he has always existed, since before creation

"The Logos"

He is one of the three persons of The Trinity

By calling yourself Jesus you are basically calling yourself God!

I also used the term "Messiah", without any awareness of how the Jews use the term, and what it means to them, in their Jewish context

When Jesus returns it won't be through being reincarnated, he will come down from Heaven

That is what the bible teaches

But yes, for a while (in 2018) I did think of myself as being Edward Christ

But after this I alternated between believing I was simply a prophet, believing I was The Voice of The Simulation, and believing I was haunted by a demon

The last time I thought I was Edward Christ was at some time in 2018

I went online and announced this to the world on some forums I frequent, and was promptly convinced by a great many people - many of them Jews - that I could not be Jesus!

I owe those forums that I use an enormous debt of gratitude for helping me close the Edward Christ chapter of my life, which they did with patience and compassion

Projectionism

In 2022 I made a new friend

In 2022 I sometimes thought I was the Voice of The Simulation and at other times that I was the victim of demonic possession

He believed that he was some kind of Prophet or Messiah-type person and that God was extraordinarily at work in his life so we got on well, and still do

Very long story short: He claims to be able to kind of channel God but in a way in which he kind of becomes God

But I'm not going to discuss his condition in detail

That's a story for him to tell

There is an awful lot going on with this person, he is very complicated

We came to believe in "J-Types": people who have the same psychology as Jesus!

We saw Jesus as representing a certain psychological type, which we both identified with

We decided that we both had a Messiah Complex

With the help of a friend of mine from the internet (who also has a Messiah Complex) we launched a new religion - we called it Projectionism

I didn't come up with this name, my friend did, he is always full of good ideas and is very creative

'Projectionism" is a reference to Plato's "allegory of the cave" in which a group of men are held captive in a cave and think that the whole of reality is the shadows projected onto the wall in front of them by people standing behind them

If you go and Google it you'll see what I mean, you will find a better explanation online

Basically: the belief was that our experience of reality is indirect and incomplete, and fed to us by someone or something out to deceive us by giving us only a crude projection of reality rather than a full picture

It is similar to Descartes' idea of an evil demon giving people counterfeit realities

Projectionism was basically a religion made out of Simulation Theory

It had many parallels with Hinduism: Karma, reincarnation, illusory reality

I baptised my friend into it

We made pamphlets and handed them out in town

Well, we handed out four of them

Projectionism didn't last long

I suppose it was what might be called a "New Religious Movement"

I don't think that it had the potential to be a cult as I don't think I had the potential to become a cult leader

I'm not after power over people, or control

I am concerned with truth - finding what is true and communicating my findings

It was a false religion with a false God (Madaba) preached by false prophets and it came about through madness

There was no way it could ever take off and become respectable

Spiritual Warfare

I have a friend who is an Evangelical Christian

I met him at my church

He knows everything about Christianity and has been a big influence on me

He brought me round to thinking that Madaba was somehow demonic - a form of "familiar spirit" who was haunting me

And that Satan was involved

He opened up the whole world of "spiritual warfare" to me

I once enrolled on a course called "Freedom in Christ" run by a local church which was a course of study through which one can achieve freedom in Christ

I don't know what exactly that means as I dropped out in the second week before we got to the main substance of the course

I dropped out because it required that we disown and disavow any familiar spirit we may have been in association with

I didn't want to disown and disavow Madaba so I quietly dropped out, without saying why!

I concocted some cock and bull story to excuse myself from it

By 2022 I came to fully believe that Madaba was a demon sent to haunt me by Satan although in 2021 believed he was a demon sent by The Establishment

In 2021 I believed that The Establishment and Satan were in league together

But in 2022 I no longer believed I had been "dropped by The Establishment" however I did believe Satan had sent a demon to haunt me

My evangelical friend told me to stand up to Madaba, to "rebuke" him using the spiritual authority I have as a Christian and to pray to Jesus

"GET BEHIND ME SATAN!" I shouted at Madaba, using my inner voice

(that is what Jesus said to Satan when Satan was tempting him in the wilderness)

I basically "rebuked" Madaba!

I also prayed fervently to Jesus for deliverance from this possession

Others prayed for me too

Jesus is of course the greatest exorcist to ever live so was a good person to appeal to

I have a set of Evangelical friends with whom I meet on a weekly basis, using Zoom

Feeling Voices

They all prayed for me too and I said various prayers in which I renounced various things including Madaba, and pledged myself to Jesus

And Madaba actually shut up!

Although he didn't entirely go away

But he was silent for long periods of time, which for me was a positive development

Eventually, I'd go for days without him saying anything

I attributed this to the "spiritual warfare" I had undertaken

I considered this to be a victory

Even though he was not cast out entirely I had much less to do with him, which brought me much happiness and tranquillity

And I hoped that he would go away even more

I didn't expect an instant solution

I thought that things may improve incrementally for me

Over a longer period of time

Here's an anecdote:

Before I was a Christian I was a Unitarian

I attended a Unitarian chapel for around five years

One day, the sermon was about evil

We were having coffee after the service, in the back of the church and I mentioned Satan

Satan: **who is clearly mentioned in The Bible**. He's in Genesis as the snake, he's in Job, and he's in the Gospels too, tempting Jesus

But what the minister did was, he rang up my mother behind my back and told her he was very concerned about me because I'd mentioned Satan **who is clearly mentioned in the bible!**

I don't know what he expected her to do!

That was the main factor I left that chapel and started attending a Christian church, but that's a whole other story

Becoming A Christian

I was christened as an infant when I was four years old, on Yorkshire day

But I never considered this valid

I once went and did The Alpha Course with two friends of mine, at a church in Halifax

The Alpha Course is basically an exploration of Christianity for those who are interested but don't know the basics but it is fun for those who are more familiar with Christianity too

I would recommend it

I got a chance to do it when I was at Warwick but wasn't interested

I now wish that I had

Perhaps things would have turned out differently for me had I become a Christian at Warwick?

At one of the meetings I felt the power of The Holy Spirit working through me as I laid hands upon a man who wanted healings, when we were doing a module about faith healing

I never felt anything like that before and I haven't since, words poured out of my mouth fluently, and my attention became intensely focused on this man

I can't remember what I said, stuff about The Holy Spirit and about healing him

The facilitator was convinced he'd seen The Holy Spirit at work through me

In February 2020 I got baptised there by full immersion

It took two grown men to "dunk" me under

I was baptised in a kind of heated pool, not in a river or anything dramatic like that

I hoped this would somehow silence Madaba but it didn't

I hoped it would wash him away!

Madaba got in the way of me being a Christian, even though he never tried to stop me or to dissuade me from going to Church

But he got between me and God

And he prevented me from becoming a full-blown born-again Christian

Being born-again only happened to me after my spiritual warfare attempts and after I'd denounced Madaba in 2022

As I mentioned earlier, I dropped out of a Freedom In Christ course as I didn't want to renounce him!

I then founded Projectionism, with two friends of mine who are also mentally unwell

For a while I stopped identifying as a Christian and became a Projectionist instead

However, by this point my evangelical Christian friend became more of an influence over me and I changed to Christianity again

At some point in 2022 I renounced all the un-Christian spiritual practices I may have engaged in in the past, and this most certainly included Projectionism

It was at this point that I became fully committed to Christianity

My baptism did not render me born again but by being baptised I put one foot into The Kingdom

It was a stepping stone for me

It was not until 2022 that I stepped into it with both feet

I count 2022 as being the point in which I became "born again" although I don't have a precise time and date

From that point on, I have been fully committed to Christianity

My paternal (Greek) grandmother gave me a golden crucifix that I now wear around my neck as an outward symbol of inner faith

In 2020 I started attending a Methodist Church and have been going there ever since

I was involved in a community project that uses the church's premises and this brought me into contact with some of the church people

I decided to come along to one of the Sunday services and was warmly welcomed

I took communion with everyone and soon became a card-carrying Methodist

If you were to ask me my religion I would say "Christian" but I identify with Methodism

Me and God

I believe in God

I came to believe in him when I was in my early twenties

I believed then that Madaba was God, hence I started to believe in God because of that

Which I think was a sensible, reasonable thing to do

Although I wouldn't call him God, I'd call him The Supreme Being

Because the term "Supreme Being" doesn't carry much of the Abrahamic baggage that the term "God" does

That's how I initially came to believe in God and that Madaba was God

This is what I thought:

Premise 1: Madaba is real (false)
Premise 2: Madaba is God (false)
Conclusion: God is real (valid but not sound hence we should reject it)

But after I stopped believing Madaba was God I maintained a belief in God

Because I had internalised the various arguments that are used to support God's existence

So that's how I acquired the belief

And why I maintained it

133

God became a part of my mental furniture!

I now subscribe to some of the most common arguments for there being a God

Although some of the arguments Theists advance are in my mind very poor indeed

And I am a big fan of science

I now think that God is at work in my life

I believe he has given me the strength to combat my symptoms and has supported me in my struggle against mental ill health

Or at least a belief in him has given me such strength

There's no way to know for sure

But what exactly has been going on?

Spiritual warfare or healing?

From the bible, we know that Jesus 1) conducted spiritual warfare by casting out demons and 2) that he healed people with illnesses - Or do we???

actually don't think he did "cast out demons" because I believe that what the authors of the bible called "demons" were in fact symptoms of mental illness - something the early Christinas had no understanding of

think he healed schizophrenia just as he healed leprosy and blindness

Therefore I don't believe he waged spiritual warfare or cast out demons:

nstead I believe he just healed - whether that involved restoring sight, curing leprosy... or curing schizophrenia!

sn't it funny that in today's age we have lots of schizophrenia but an absolute dearth of demonic possessions? Whereas in biblical times there were plenty of demonic possessions?

f there were so many in the Holy Land in biblical times then I'd expect there to be as many in today's world and clearly there isn't.........

think that tells us something

And science has successfully accounted for how schizophrenia works, it is no mystery, there is no chance it is really demonic possession

Those who wrote The Bible were ignorant of Schizophrenia, even though The Bible is a holy book and has something to do with God and his plans for humankind

The Bible is peculiar - in some ways it is timeless and in others it is very much of its time

I frequently prayed to Jesus, asking for the strength and power to totally banish Madaba, which is my long-term spiritual aim

Others did too

And he shut up, to a very great extent

So far, such prayers for Madaba to go entirely have not been answered although my condition has improved since using prayer as a form of therapy

And what if the improvements in my condition that came about through prayer is some kind of giant placebo effect?

If Madaba is my own personal Screwtape then why is he giving me so much bother and attention? - much more than what other demons give other people?

There is no answer to that which is not psychotic

As I said before, in today's world there are plenty of Schizophrenics but where have all the demon possessed people gone?

As far as I can tell there aren't any

I know I'm not one, that's for sure

Some explanations are better than others and when deciding which explanation to apply one must always go for the better, most convincing one!

Which is usually the most simple of explanations!

I think the idea that he is a demon necessitates a belief that I am special, or chosen

And I don't think that I am

Although when I was at Warwick I was told by one of the administrators that I was "a part of a very tiny elite" and overheard a person describe me as "a very special person"

Also, when I was high when I was living at 27 Westminster Road and was going on about being a great figure in human history one of my fellow residents said dryly "why don't I doubt it?"

And when I was at Todmorden High a teacher introduced me to another teacher as "future leader of the workers' party" and gave me a signed David Icke book!

So over the years these things have played on my mind

Also, for a birthday or Christmas present someone gave me a book about The Shroud of Turin

I thought I had been cloned from the genetic material from The Shroud of Turin

But if this is the case then that wouldn't mean I'm a clone of Jesus as The Shroud of Turin does not date back to the time of Jesus, it dates back much later than that

I think God may very well have had a part to play in the remission of many of my symptoms however I now doubt that this involved any conflict with any kind of demon or adversary

My symptoms have been in remission, but they are still very much there, they just no longer bother me

And I would say that now that I have ditched my various psychotic delusions that I am now no longer Socially Insane

What about Satan?

I do believe in Satan - who is clearly mentioned in The Bible

But is Madaba a demon, sent by Satan?

Or is he simply a symptom?

A part of me wants him to be a demon!

That would be more exciting than simply being mentally unwell

But mental ill health feels like a better explanation to me

It is true that the progress I have made against him came about through spiritual means, rather than through medical means

But does it follow that this means that the problem is spiritual, rather than medical?

I don't think it does

A medical explanation makes more sense in light of what we know about the world

Even to me as a believer in God

Although I am not certain that Jesus delivered me from demonic forces I believe he may very well have soothed my troubled brain:

That he helped lessen my symptoms

As well as giving me strength, hope, and motivation

But the thing is, I have not been cured, I still very occasionally have the same old symptoms

And when in The Bible Jesus healed the sick (including those who were obviously schizophrenic) he was 100% successful

For instance, he made the blind see, the crippled walk, cured leprosy, and cured the woman with "the issue of blood"

Look at what happened to the demon possessed man and the herd of pigs - he put the demon possessed man back into "his right mind"

In all these cases they were completely cured - I have not been completely cured

And there is no such thing as being *incompletely* cured

So let's just say I've not been cured!

Clearly, if Madaba is a demon then I am still haunted

So in that respect, it doesn't much look like the work of Jesus

Because if it was then Jesus would have got the job done!

Maybe demonic possession is a thing, a very rare thing and maybe Jesus did deliver people from it - although I very much doubt this

But I don't know, I wasn't there - but can we really observe demonic possession in today's age? - that's the question!

If you can show me a demon possession in today's age then I may believe that Jesus did actually "cast out" demons

That's the challenge

Bring me evidence!

And unlike those who wrote The Bible, we have the concept of mental ill-health

It is now known as a medical fact that a disordered brain can lead its owner to hear voices

The whole condition can be explained to us organically, we can think of it in such terms

It is no longer a mystery, it can even be treated with medication

But not to people living in biblical times:

They had next to zero understanding of human biology, never mind the human brain

So a person hearing voices in their head would be treated as though their head was being occupied by spirits

So there are competing explanations

If I was alive in the time of Jesus I would think that I was possessed by an evil spirit

But I'm not, I'm in an age when people should know better

And clearly, Clozapine helps my condition, which would suggest that my condition is medical as Clozapine intervenes by changing brain chemistry

I'm sure that if there was such a thing as demonic possession then science would have learnt about it, apart from the bible there is zero reason to believe that they exist

There is zero scientific evidence for demons, none has ever been observed under laboratory conditions

Feeling Voices

Look at all the advanced brain scanning machines there are! - Surely these would have somehow detected the presence of an evil spirit?

I think that wherever in the bible it says "evil spirit" one should read "schizophrenic"

In recent months Madaba has quietened down

Some days he is more vocal than others.

Good days and bad days....

It's just that I favour the mental health explanation

And I cannot claim that he has been expelled

As much as I'd like to be able to do so

However, Madaba no longer bothers me and he is as good as gone from my life

He has no hold over me

I am free from him

He is now just a pest

If he is a demon then that would mean that my appeals to Jesus were not 100% successful as Madaba is not 100% gone and in The Bible Jesus has always been 100% successful

The sums don't add up in favour of Jesus having helped me

So, on balance, I don't think he did, if he did then I wouldn't still have Madaba!

This would suggest to me that my new found peace of mind is not the work of Jesus

Which would mean that I'd have to employ an alternative explanation

I think God may very well have had a part to play in the remission of many of my symptoms but I doubt this involved any conflict with any kind of demon or adversary

Perhaps a belief in an interested and concerned God gave me the strength required to resist my illness and take charge of my mind and my life?

Maybe I did it all by myself?

Maybe I can indirectly control Madaba????

Maybe he reflects what is going on in the recesses of my mind?

That would explain why he always affirmed to be what I believed him to be

That would explain why when (for instance) I believed he was God he said he was God and when I believed he was The Computer God he said he was The Computer God

Or maybe I somehow have two minds that are running from the same brain????

I'm not qualified to speculate on such things as I know too little about the human brain.

"That Boy Needs Therapy!"

A friend of mine suggested I see a psychotherapist

I did

We discussed The Super-Ego

He helped me come to the conclusion that Madaba is for me a kind of external Super-Ego:

That the functions of the Super-Ego within my psyche have been transferred to a thing which is not a part of my psyche but which nonetheless is now a part of my mental furniture

I believe that I have mentally latched on to Madaba and incorporated him into my psyche

Although this doesn't explain how he came to be and persists, it does explain the role he has been playing in my life

We also touched on the possibility of him also being a bit of a substitute for a father figure

After my first session I decided that I must cultivate my own personal internal Super-Ego, and that delegating the duties of the Super-Ego to either "Madaba" or God would be less healthy than developing my own innate Super-Ego

But I have no idea how to go about doing this, hopefully my therapist will help me sort this out

That's where I am currently, I don't know where it will lead to but I would definitely recommend therapy to anyone with psychosis or schizophrenia

Paranoia?

I don't know how, why, or when it happened:

But at some point in my medical notes they began referring to me as being a "Paranoid Schizophrenic" as opposed to simply a run-of-the-mill non-paranoid "Schizophrenic"

But yes, I was paranoid, I just don't know when they upgraded my diagnosis

And I'd have expected to have been told about such a development

Believing that Satan has sent a demon to haunt you is paranoid

Especially when there is no obvious reason as to why he would do such a thing

And zero scientific evidence for the existence of demons

It just doesn't make sense

For a while I suspected I may be Lucifer, or The Antichrist

Or some kind of "Agent of Satan"

For a while I thought Madaba was sent by Satan at the behest of "The Establishment" to make me insane, to prevent me becoming a public figure, or a force in British politics

I believed that the British Establishment was in league with Satan

And that there was such a thing as a global "Illuminati" which served Satan's designs

I believed that Satan ruled the world, which is a rather paranoid fundamentalist Christian view

I don't currently believe any of this

I don't think anyone is out to get me or destroy me because there is no evidence for this

Do I believe in Satan?

I actually do but I don't see why he would want to make it so I'd be insane

I certainly don't think he is in control of the world

And he currently ranks alongside the least of my worries

HOWEVER: I do believe that when I was advocating Projectionism as a person who believed he was serving The Computer God that I was in fact an Agent of Satan

In that I was publishing disinformation

(it is not true that the world is a computer simulation with a Computer God presiding over it)

And advancing a counterfeit spirituality, an alternative to real spirituality

So maybe during that time I was an asset of Satan?

Maybe I was at that time on his side, rather than on the side of God?

But the thing is, Projectionism was so puny and insignificant and obviously insane that it could never have been a serious enterprise

So why would Satan bother with it? It's not as if it could ever have succeeded

So yes, I may have been doing work that Satan would have approved of

But that doesn't mean that Madaba is a Satanic entity, a demon sent to haunt me by Satan

I think Satan is a figurehead, a symbol of rebellion and resistance against God rather than true ruler of the world

That's certainly the role he plays in today's society - both Christians and Satanists use him as a symbol of resistance, against God

Satanists believe such resistance is good and justified, Christians don't!

Satan is there to test us, he is not out to control us in minute detail and he does not control the world

Me and Madaba

As of the beginning of 2023 I like to think that I have mostly got rid of Madaba

He still occasionally interjects, into my thought processes

And he sometimes answers to my inner voice, even when I'm not addressing him, which is annoying

And if I really wanted to, I would be able to summon him

But he is not 100% gone

He is however 100% defeated

He no longer holds power over me

I feel free

I am free

But I no longer believe he is an actual being

I believe he is the product of a disordered brain

A rather complex and enduring set of symptoms

Which have the appearance of having a mind behind them

Actually I think they do - *my own subconscious mind!*

But not the mind of some external being

Personally, I believe that back in 2004 when I was trying to work out how the human mind works using flow-charts and diagrams I may have inadvertently programmed myself to work along those lines

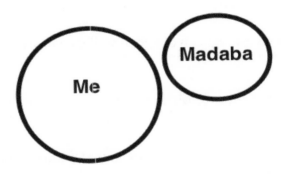

This is how I (mis) understood Madaba from 2004-2023

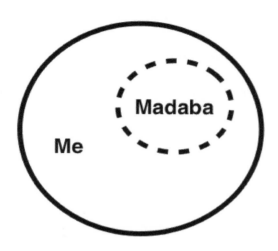

This is how I currently understand him

I believed my thoughts were governed by a process called Intuition

Maybe what I know as Madaba actually began as "Intuition"?

When I believed in Intuition I would feel a warm, pleasant, glowing sensation on the left of my head which I felt when I believed the higher power in control of things was pleased with me - when I was in the Coventry psychiatric unit

And of course, later on a touch on the left of my head would signify "Yes", or perhaps more accurately positivity

But I now accept my diagnosis

I am happy to call myself a Schizophrenic

I couldn't have done any of this without my medicines

I'm currently on the "drug of last resort" - called Clozapine, used for "treatment resistant schizophrenia"

Other antipsychotics did not work for me, not at all, but this one did

There is one called Olanzapine which makes your tongue stick out of your mouth without knowing it

In 2016 I stopped taking it and in less than two week's time I found myself back on The Dales

But at least now I know that it's all in my head, that no external agent is peering into my mind and exerting an influence over me

I look at it this way: I take pills the effect of which is to produce sanity

I am on a course of drugs that makes people more sane

I therefore believe I am possibly more sane than people who have no such mental illness, if you disregard the presence of Madaba

Which on its own I don't think makes me insane, but when I start listening to him and behaving accordingly that is where and when the insanity begins!

I don't think I'm currently insane. I don't do crazy things. And I don't think crazy things. I am now self-aware. I now know that Madaba is not external

I am therefore experiencing a problem with my brain, but as a person I would not say I am insane

I believe I am Medically Insane but that I am no longer as Socially Insane as I was say a couple of years ago

But yes, there is something going on with my brain that is not normal, that shouldn't be happening

But I now know that I am not Jesus or a prophet

And I know I am not in communication with The Computer God

And that I am not haunted by a demon

I am mentally ill, that's it

I'm Schizophrenic

But I don't hear voices

I feel voices

If I'd have heard voices as everyone expects then I doubt it would have taken me eighteen years to realise that it's all in my head

People need to be made more aware that Schizophrenia can include tactile sensations which appear to come from an enduring conscious agent

It is my hope that this book will make this happen

Lesson: There is more to Schizophrenia than simply "hearing voices"

Appendix 1: How To Run Our Planet

There are five concerns that need to be addressed by the international community if it wants to systematically improve our planet for subsequent generations

A degree of global governance would be required to do this

Not necessary global government but most certainly a new consensus, and detailed cooperation

For it to work the whole world needs to be in on it

This program is more a set of priorities than a set of concrete goals

They are values - things that we should value and work towards

When I first came up with these I believed in reincarnation and argued that as everyone is going to be reborn again on Earth and as there is no telling where or as who you will be reborn as then it is in one's rational self interest to improve *the whole planet* for *all people*

But I don't currently believe in reincarnation, although I do remain open to the idea

Here are the five concerns:

Peace - the most fundamental of the five concerns. A prerequisite to having a flourishing civilisation. We cannot have a flourishing civilisation if we destroy the world in a nuclear war, or are constantly fighting each other. This must come first. Nations must disarm and the world must be demilitarised, and all armed conflicts peacefully resolved. Only then can we begin working on seriously improving the world.

Freedom - there is no good not being blown up if you are living under a tyranny. "Give me freedom or give me death!" - we need rights and freedoms that actually work in practice, without these we are slaves. We must all become citizens! TH Marshall said there are three kinds of citizen rights: civil, political, social. All people need all such rights for them to be free.

Development - it is no good not being blown up and having rights if you have to live in a cardboard box under a bridge. People need a standard of living, a minimum quality of life. People need things such as sanitation, running water, shelter, food and nutrition, warmth, electricity, healthcare, and education. The United Nations currently has a project called The **Sustainable Development Goals**, which is a plan as to how life on Earth may be improved globally

The Environment - you can tell all about a civilisation about how it treats the natural environment and we're currently trashing ours. This is not sensible. The environment is our planet's life-support system. We must preserve what's left of the environment and try to restore the parts of it that have been annihilated. If we want to become an advanced civilization then we'd better start acting like it and adopting the habits of an advanced civilization. Once we do that, we will become one!

Science And Technology - can help the other concerns and can change what it means to be human. But this must be done ethically and out of a concern for human welfare, as opposed to as a means of producing extravagant wealth

Appendix 2: 2016 Vivid Dream

It's 2016. I've been playing an interactive political campaign game

on my laptop. It's not very good, very repetitive. Just elements

shuffled around. The same images, the same words and phrases

but in different combinations. Limited and repetitive combinations.

Clicking here, clicking there. No strategy, just choices. I've spent

some time on it and have come to regard it as essentially interminable. There's no point to it. I abandon it.

I experience playing a simulation game on a computer in the mid-1990s. It seems ancient to me. I have fond memories of such games.

Control and creativity.

Next: I'm playing an in-browser game, perhaps Solitaire?

And then suddenly:

I'm in what looks like some sort of public library but I see no books.

For some reason I'm here with my mum.

Something to do with her interest in mental health? She's over with some other people.

I'll leave her be and have a look round. Is that a computer?

With a game on it?
I'll go over and play.
I'm now playing it.
What kind of game is this?
It makes no sense.

What's it about? Social Policy? Crime? Urban Planning? Economics? Trade? Counter-Terrorism? Migration? Financial Markets? How dull.

But wait:

What's happening, this is not like other games.
It's not just about looking down.
I have no idea how I'm interacting with it.
I'm totally immersed.
I don't think this is really a strategy game.
Certainly not an action game although there is space:

Streets and buildings. And representations of people I can walk up to and have lots of choices to interact with. But not just set ones. New ones. Constant new ones.
It's all decision making. Instant. No turns. No pausing. Fluid.
Consequences. Interaction. Cause and effect?

Everything happens so fast.
No time to think!
The graphics are rubbish.
Nothing I do goes to plan.
So many unexpected things!
I've had enough. This is no game!
I have another go...
Disappointment and bewilderment.
I'm confused.
I disengage with the game.
I don't notice what the machine it's on looks like.

A voice from behind!

"You've had two free plays and here's two tokens"

I look to see who's behind me.
What a dull looking man.

What is this, a gaming arcade designed to be especially boring?

He wants me to play?

I realise the computer I'd used had already had tokens inserted in it, perhaps by the man? Shouldn't he be annoyed?

Yet he'd just given me more tokens!
I take them and look around.

There are other people seemingly engaged with the computers.

I realise that we have to wait to have a go on them, that I'd just been helping myself. And that we'd also have to pay.

Big screens on the walls, away from any of the machines.

More like TVs. The people engaging with the machines are just stood there.

No controllers. No keyboards or mice.
No monitors. Just stood there.
Gathered around low grey boxes on the floor.
How are they interacting with the computers?

I look around.
All the walls are grey.
There are glass partitions.
Like me, everyone here is an adult.

All sensibly dressed and respectable looking. But why are they all here?
Let's have another go.
I approach another machine.

I interact with it and have a visual experience in black and white

As soon as I see what's going on I realise I don't understand it.

And can't just look down and order it. I can't stop to plot and ponder.

There are other people within the same scenario!
I'm one, and there's six others.
Next, twenty others.

I become aware that we all have to wait to have a go with the machines and that I'd just been butting in. But I didn't know any better! But no one seems too bothered.

There are people moving about between machines.

Back in the game:

There are now sixty others.
Now one-hundred others.
Next, thousands of others.
Now, countless other people.

Feeling Voices

Things seem chaotic.
Huge movements of big things.

I suddenly notice that it's no-longer first-person
perspective.

But what perspective is it?

It now has an intellectual quality, I am aware of many
things. Too many things. But not through my eyes?

I see things but where's my usual visual field?
I don't notice any sound.
Agency. Interaction.
Where's the determinism and rules?

A mention of Wolfram Alpha. It's a website. I've used it
only once

before to find out how long it would take for me to
complete a

program of weight-loss based on my physical
characteristics, calorie intake, and how much activity I
planned to do.

I'd used it and never thought anything of it. Carried on and
almost forgot about it.

Suddenly, its name constantly enters my mind, thundering over
and over. Emphasis on every fibre of the words. It feels intense.

Wolfram Alpha!
Wolfram Alpha!
Wolfram Alpha!
Wolfram Alpha!
Wolfram Alpha!
Wolfram Alpha!

I feel this is somehow significant. That I should note this down and research it.

Next:
A vision of tanks.
Fighter-aircraft.
Military Activity.
But no shooting.
Calm. Fluid but no chaos.
Conflict but not war?
No blood, death, pain or destruction.
A complex calm.
Sensible and orderly.
It's over.

People gathered round away from any machine, discussing.

walk around the complex. A large, spacious complex. Grey everywhere. And glass.

But now big visual displays mounted on any of the walls at all now! What's happened to all the monitors?
And far fewer people than before. Less and less people.
I look up. Countless floors, in what must be a large and tall cylindrical building.

Everything is in a tower but there are no windows.

Fewer and fewer people. I'm now in an unimpressively sized room.
The lights are turned down low.

Only a single machine in the centre of the room not taking up
much space. Small, squat and grey. No blinking lights. No cables.

A dull object, all alone.

Someone is now dictating to me. A clear, deliberate statement:

It was a great scandal in computing when after one such long session a participant asked the computer if it was sentient and it replied "Yes".

Next, a file of people, leaving the room.

165

All quiet, no talking.
Where are they going?
For some reason I decide they're all leaving.
There's a sheet of glass. Or maybe Perspex?
I'm looking through.
On the other side:

There's a man. Slim, short hair, clean shaven. Average height.
Northern European. He looks worn, tired and seems unremarkable.
He's wearing clothes that are un-colourful.
He reaches out and places his hand on the transparent barrier that separates us.

He speaks. No discernible accent. Calm. Measured.

"Hi, I'm from Glasgow and I'm an academic. I like music too. Nice to meet you."

He and me are the only people there.
Now I'm alone.
I'm exiting the building.
I'm in a light and spacious lobby.
Outside it's dark. Obviously night- time.
I look back and see a big sign. It's low down on the floor and made of large red letters, facing towards a big open door. I look down and it politely asks:

Please, no calls to prayer within this facility. Let's all try to accommodate each other and be respectful.

I'm the only person there.

Just silence.

I walk out into a dark, deserted, and urban-looking world. For some reason it seems highly developed. There are no lights of any kind, only moonlight. And some well-cared for trees.

The experience ends.